Where to
Walk Your Dog
in
Greater Vancouver

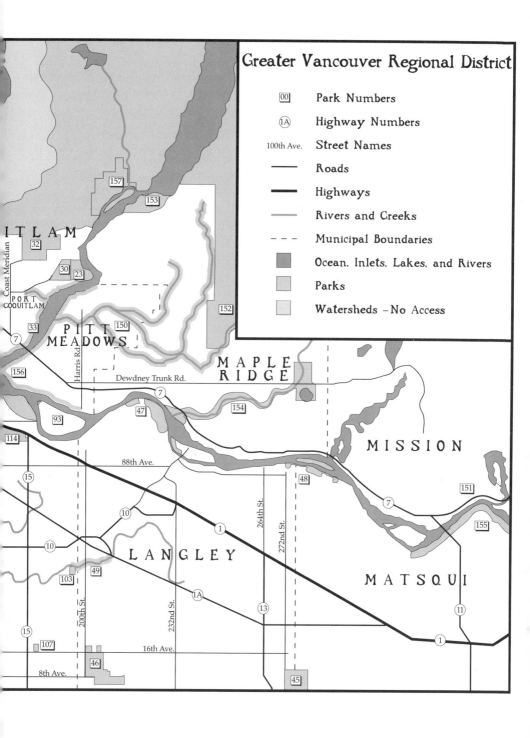

Greater Vancouver Regional District

00	Park Numbers
1A	Highway Numbers
100th Ave.	Street Names
——	Roads
——	Highways
——	Rivers and Creeks
- - -	Municipal Boundaries
▓	Ocean, Inlets, Lakes, and Rivers
▒	Parks
░	Watersheds – No Access

ITLAM

157

153

32

Coast Meridian

30 23

PORT COQUITLAM

152

33

7

PITT MEADOWS

150

Harris Rd.

MAPLE RIDGE

156

Dewdney Trunk Rd.

7

154

47

93

114

88th Ave.

MISSION

15

48

151

10

7

155

10

LANGLEY

49

103

264th St.

272nd St.

1

MATSQUI

200th St.

232nd St.

1A

13

11

15

1

107

16th Ave.

46

45

8th Ave.

Where to
Walk Your Dog
in
Greater Vancouver

by

Ross W. Powell
and
Hero

Arcadian Productions
Vancouver

Canadian Cataloguing In Publication Data
Powell, Ross W. (Ross Warren), 1957–
  Where to walk your dog in Greater Vancouver

Includes index.
ISBN 0-9683117-0-9

  1. Dog walking—British Columbia—Greater Vancouver—Guidebooks. 2. Trails—British Columbia—Greater Vancouver—Guidebooks. 3. Greater Vancouver (BC)—Guidebooks. I. Title.
SF427.46.P68 1998   636.7'0887'0971133   C98-910667-5

Published in Canada by
Arcadian Productions Inc.
PO Box # 54055
1562 Lonsdale Avenue
V7M 3L5
PH: (604) 988-3679
FX: (604) 986-0646
E-mail: Arcadia@istar.ca

Distributed by **Gordon Soules Book Publishers Ltd**. ● 1359 Ambleside Lane, West Vancouver, BC, Canada V7T 2Y9 ● PMB 620, 1916 Pike Place #12, Seattle, WA 98101-1097 US
E-mail: books@gordonsoules.com
Web site: http://www.gordonsoules.com
(604) 922 6588 Fax: (604) 688 5442

Visit our web page at;
http://home.istar.ca/~arcadia/walkyourdog.html

Cover photograph of Mosquito Creek by Marcel Williams.
All other photographs and all maps by Ross W. Powell.
Pencil drawing of Spooky by Robert Powell.
Design by Harry Bardal and Ross W. Powell.
Printed and bound in Canada by Hignell Printing Ltd.

This book is dedicated to

Spooky

Powell '72

1965 - 1980

for all the great times we had
mucking about down the creek.

Table of Contents

Photographs

Maps

Disclaimer

This book is intended as a general guide to parks in the Greater Vancouver Regional District and not as a primer in wilderness outdoorsmanship. Users of this guidebook assume responsibility for their own safety, including evaluating whether their health and physical condition, as well as their outdoor travel training and experience, are appropriate for any given hike.

Information in any guidebook is subject to change and error. In addition, this guidebook does not list all possible hazards or describe conditions as they may be encountered on any particular day nor does it describe all by-laws and regulations relating to pets in every area. Readers hold the ultimate and sole responsibility to be aware of changes inpark regulations, conditions, hazards, and by-laws and regulations relating to their pets which might have occurred since the writing of this book. Neither the author, Ross W. Powell, nor the publisher, Arcadian Productions Inc., shall have any liability or responsibility to any person or animals with respect to any loss or damage caused or alleged to be caused directly or indirectly by information contained in this guidebook.

Errors and Omissions

In any guidebook, the information is subject to change and error. The authors would be grateful for any corrections our readers might have to the current text, or suggestions for ways in which future editions might be made better, as well as any parks or trails we might have missed.

Please send all comments and suggestions in care of;

Arcadian Productions Inc.
PO Box # 54055
1562 Lonsdale Avenue
North Vancouver, BC
V7M 3L5
PH: (604) 988-3679
FX: (604) 986-0646
E-mail: Arcadia@istar.ca

Visit our web page at;
http://home.istar.ca/~arcadia/walkyourdog.html

Acknowledgments

I would like to thank the Parks Board of BC, the GVRD Parks Department and the Parks Departments of all the municipalities in Greater Vancouver for their support and help in this project.

Thanks to Marion Crook, author of *How to Self Publish and Make Money*, for all her excellent advice. Thanks to Gordon Soules of Gordon Soules Book Publishers for his keen interest and advice. Thanks also to Sharman King, owner of the Book Warehouse chain, for his advice.

Thanks to Colleen Anderson for copy editing and proofreading.

Thanks to Michael Wilson, Charm Cottingham, Cindy and Willie Ferguson, and Rob and Kilby Cottingham MacBean for reading the early versions. Thanks to Michelle Penney and Brenda Longland for showing up to PA on the photo-shoots (talk about your idling Porsches). Thanks also to my brother, Mark Powell, for coming walkies, for the scans, and for launching our web page. Thanks to my other brother, Robert Powell, for the drawing of our old dog, Spooky, and to my sister, Janet Powell, for the last minute copy editing.

Thanks to Jane Christy for breeding and raising Hero and allowing us to adopt him. Thanks to Greta and Lorne Hanis for all the fabulous neighbourly help and advice on dog rearing.

Special thanks to Willie Ferguson for all the great company and scintillating conversation on the trail.

I would especially like to thank my wife and my partner in Arcadian Productions, Nancy Cottingham Powell, for supporting me in every way and believing in this project, as she does in all my projects.

Hero would like to thank Kira, Sage, and Willow (Hanis), and especially his girlfriend Bessie (Ferguson).

Introduction

This book contains detailed information on hundreds of places to walk your dog in the Greater Vancouver Regional District, from everyday walks in your neighbourhood, through slightly more adventurous day trips, right up to wilderness treks.

One of the amazing things about researching this book was discovering all the incredible places there are to visit in the GVRD. I grew up in Vancouver and have lived here for 40 years. I thought I'd been just about everywhere worth going to in the Greater Vancouver area. I was so very wrong. My travels took me to fabulous parks I never knew existed, right in our own back yard.

Owning a dog in suburbia is quite different than it was when I was a kid. My parents' dog ran wild, everybody's did. We let him out when he wanted and he cruised the neighbourhood until he was ready to come home. Dogs in those days had their regular route that they walked every day, consisting of a few square blocks and some other dogs that they visited. As kids we did much the same–I was allowed to disappear into the woods, all by myself, though almost invariably with dog in tow, from the time I was old enough to go to school. Nowadays we accompany our dogs and our offspring everywhere they go, and so in these days of urban expansion we need our parks more than ever.

The GVRD is getting more and more crowded and parkland more scarce with every house and condo built. Land that used to be unused bush is being put to some use or another, which has the effect of squeezing everyone into using the few remaining parcels of land for recreation. What can you do about it, you say?

Get involved in the parks planning in your municipality and the GVRD. Lend your support to campaigns to create more parks. If you want lots of places with enough room to accommodate dog walking and especially off-leash walking then you had better help make sure that those wild lands that do still exist are preserved. Call and write the various levels of parks boards in your area and tell them that you want more designated off-leash dog walking areas. See the appendix for the contact numbers at the Parks and Recreation Departments in your area.

In researching and writing this book I went to a great many places in Greater Vancouver that I had never visited before. If you let it, this book will help you become more familiar with this great corner of the world. I hope everyone who reads this book will gain a great deal of happiness from the wonderful places to which it can lead you.

Hero says; "...and your dogs too!"

General

I have concentrated the focus of the walks and hikes in this book in the areas of greatest urban intensity–the city of Vancouver and its immediate surroundings. The number of entries in any given area also reflects the number of parks in which dog walking is an option, as well as how much information there was available from that municipality. Some walks have been included in the outlying areas of Greater Vancouver for those people who live there, as well as for those intrepid city folk who want to get out and see new things. Inevitably, there will be good parks I have left out and trails that I have missed. I would be happy to hear from anyone with suggestions for future editions of this book.

Please note that not all of the parks I review in this book are parks that I recommend as especially good dog-walking parks. Rather than do a selective "101 Dog Walks," I decided that folks would like to be warned off the bad parks as well as apprised of the good ones. When one looks at a street map, the green square that designates a park doesn't give one much to go on. Many parks were left out, however, because they were just one of hundreds that were entirely inappropriate, and were not one of the "major" parks that people might be inclined to check out on their own. Well, I went there, I checked them out, and I'll tell you about it so you don't have to go to the boring ones.

To facilitate easy browsing, a set of icons for each entry will tell you at a glance what sort of park you are going to, as well as some point-form information on how long the walk is, how difficult, and the general condition of the trail. Hero and I have then rated our enjoyment of the walk. I have included a brief write-up that will tell you what sort of park it is, as well as any hazards (watch for the word "WARNING" in the text) or special considerations that walking the park may entail.

There is much to say about many of the parks found in Greater Vancouver, in regards to their natural history as well as human history, the current uses, and any heritage buildings they contain, etc. However, comments are limited to the ways in which the parks impact upon you, the walker, and your dog, lest this book become unwieldy. Many of the municipalities in which these parks exist and in particular the GVRD have pamphlets on their parks that will further enlighten those who are interested.

How To Use This Book

This section describes how the book is laid out, what information you may expect to find, as well as how to most easily access that information.

Municipalities are arranged alphabetically in chapters, and the parks are arranged in alphabetic order within their municipality. The parks are numbered sequentially throughout the book and these numbers are displayed on the GVRD master map at the front of the book, as well as similar maps at the chapter head of each municipality. This will show you at a glance where parks in any given area are located.

The Icons

The icons listed below will give you some idea of the amenities available in each park or by each trail. Please note that most of the amenities are clustered at the beginning of the trails.

Please also note that, very occasionally, the icons listed may differ from the official planned use of an area and should not be taken to grant accessibility to an area for a particular activity. E.g. I have listed biking when I encountered a lot of cyclists. Sometimes this is in an area where biking is prohibited and I am listing it to make walkers aware of the hazard.

 Off-Leash Areas　　　　　 Planned rezoning pending

Most municipalities in Greater Vancouver have laws that state dogs must be leashed at all times when on public land. Off-leash zonings are currently in a state of flux in most municipalities so watch for changes.

Parks which receive the icon of the dog happily wagging his tail (you can see this if you look really closely) have areas which have been designated as Off-Leash Areas. Please consult the text for exactly which areas have been so designated.

Dogs off-leash must be kept under your control at all times, of course. Please note that this means keeping the dog from running ahead on the trail if this takes him out of your sight.

 Dogs Prohibited

This park contains places where your dog is prohibited. Even when there is no signage to this effect, dogs are routinely barred from playgrounds, sports fields, most beaches, fitness circuits, picnic areas, running tracks, tennis courts, bowling greens, etc. You get the picture. Use your common sense. Just because bocci courts are not described in the official list, don't think your dog is welcome there.

Water

This symbol denotes the presence of bodies of water as opposed to water out of the tap; creeks, rivers, the ocean, lakes, ponds, ditches, and large puddles. Your dog is not always allowed in said water, particularly at beaches and in streams when fish are spawning.

Where the data was available to me I have included a water quality rating from the *British Columbia Water Status Report*, using the "general" water quality index; Excellent, Good, Fair, Borderline, Poor. Note that water quality is changeable.

 Telephone

This icon denotes that public telephones are available in the park or at the trailhead. It does not cover private telephones in nearby buildings that could be used in an emergency.

 Washroom

This symbol designates public washrooms. Often these will be at the picnic area next to the parking lot, and miles from where you are when you need them. Please note that many washrooms close for the winter. (What? People don't have to pee when it's cold?)

 Drinking Water

This symbol denotes a source of drinking (tap) water. Please note that many taps are turned off for the winter. Always carry drinking water on longer walks, especially when it is hot.

Never drink from outside (natural) water sources. No matter how clear and clean the water looks, and no matter how delicious it tastes, it is inadvisable to drink from any body of water, including fresh mountain streams, without first boiling or filtering the water, (with an approved filter system, not a coffee filter), or adding an approved water purifier. A dead animal out of sight upstream could infect the water with any number of parasites or diseases. Even your dog will pick these up from time to time and its resistance to such things is much higher.

 Handicap Access

Often when a park lists Handicap Access in a brochure they are referring to the fact that a wheelchair can be off-loaded into a picnic area and that there are wheelchair accessible washrooms. Since almost all picnic areas are off-limits to dogs, I have included this icon only when I deem that the average person in a wheelchair might actually be able to get into the park and have somewhere to go with their dog. Even so, Handicap Access usually applies to only a portion of the trails listed.

 Biking

When this symbol appears the trails have either been designated for biking, or we have noticed that the trails are frequented by cyclists, even though this may not be the planned use. This usually means that hikers and their dogs are also welcome. The intensity of the ride will be noted by the Trail Difficulty rating.

 Jogging

Some of these will be formal running tracks and others are places I have seen people jogging, or even trails I just feel would be good to jog on. I don't jog, myself.

 Swimming

The swimming symbol may be used to note park areas officially designated for this use in natural bodies of water. It does not cover such facilities as swimming pools where your dog is not allowed. It may also be used to denote those places where people go swimming, like some little lakes up the mountains. Note that most beaches are off-limits to your dog, especially in the summer.

 Horses

Paths may be designated multiple use and often horses are included. Use your common (horse) sense and your knowledge of your own dog to determine whether or not these trails are suitable for you. Certainly, it is imperative to keep your dog from rushing up to horses, even joyfully, as you do not know the temperament of the horse nor the level of expertise of the rider.

 Fishing

Fishing may well be possible in areas other than those noted in this book. Only places that were recommended to me as good fishing spots, or places I witnessed people fishing, have been noted. The relevance for nonfishing dog walkers is, of course, that you don't want to annoy fishermen by letting your dog jump into the water right where they have their line.

Trail Difficulty

Trail difficulty is basically an indication of how much climbing is involved in the hike, or the steepness of the trail.

1 - Completely level walk on a nice flat trail.

2 - Mostly level walk, some minor ups and downs.

3 - Slightly steep, some climbing involved.

4 - Quite steep, definite climbing involved. Good aerobic activity.

5 - Major climbing. Very steep. Probably some areas where you might have to climb using your hands on the rock, and maybe haul your dog up by his collar. Think carefully about how well your dog climbs before you attempt this, always knowing, however, that Hero was able to make it.

Trail Condition

Trail condition is an indicator of how well groomed a trail is. It takes into account things like the amount of mud on the trail, tree roots you have to clamber over, loose gravel or rocks, as well as whether the foliage is trimmed back or not.

Excellent - A flat, smooth trail, usually of gravel or bark mulch, highly groomed and regularly maintained.

Good - A well-traveled trail with few rocks or roots, but generally an even smooth surface.

Fair - A trail with an uneven surface, rocks and roots to step over, possibly creeks to cross, but one that is looked after by the park or a hiking club.

Rustic - A trail which might be a bit more trouble to traverse. Lots of uneven ground. Probably in a wilderness park, and has been more or less created by use.

Poor - Denotes what is essentially a deer trail; a trail that has been created by use, often overgrown and unreliable. You're on your own and better have good boots, and a compass if it's out in the wilderness.

Time

This one is the trickiest. People travel at markedly different speeds. Many parks have a tangle of trails which one could loop through quickly or wander in circles forever. Linear trails are often so long that you are reduced to walking out until you feel you are half way, then walking back.

I have tried therefore, to give a sense of how much walking time is available in a park.

For specific trails within a park, unless otherwise noted, all times are based on return time; the time it might take you to walk the trail and get back again, either retracing your steps or coming back on the other side of a loop trail. Once you have done a few walks in the book, you will know how to gauge your walking time with ours, which tends to be a bit faster than average.

The Trail Reviews

Each trail or park has a short descriptive write-up covering what sort of walk you are going to encounter; whether a mountainous trail, a seaside park, a walk on open dykes or through thick forest, as well as any remarkable things about the park.

You will come across the term "deer trail" in this book. I'm not sure how prevalent this term is, but I have always understood it to mean a very minor trail that has been worn through the bush by feet, as opposed to one properly cut through the bush and maintained. It refers to trails that are less established than the main trails in any given area.

The Rating System

Hero's Rating: 🐾 🐾 🐾 🐾 🐾

Hero's ratings (from 1 to 5 paws) are necessarily taken from his perspective and will be good or bad depending on certain things which Hero likes.

Hero is not a stick dog, he's not a ball dog, he's not a rock dog, and for a Golden Retriever, he's not much into retrieving. Hero is a social dog; he loves to meet people and other dogs. Hero is a water dog; he loves to paddle in the ocean, lakes, streams, and puddles. Hero is a walking dog and this, especially when it involves trails in the woods, he loves more than anything in the world. More than digging holes in the back yard. More than slobbering on the cats.

People who read this book will invariably be "dog people" and "dog people" are interested in such things. I also tell you these things so that you will know where Hero is coming from in his ratings, and you will be able to judge accordingly how these ratings will match the temperament of your dog.

Hero tends to give an extra paw to any place with water, Off-Leash Areas, other dogs, and to places with great smells. He will take a paw away if a park is too noisy or urban. Hero likes big parks because he likes to go for long walks.

Hero's girlfriend, Bessie, will occasionally put her two cents worth in as well.

Human's Rating: ★ ★ ★ ★ ★

As with Hero's ratings, I could only do this from a personal perspective (from 1 to 5 stars). I like scenery, and this is probably the most important factor. Whether it's a beautiful forest, an inspiring view, or a lovely marsh, this is mainly what draws me to a particular park. I am not at all concerned with amenities like concessions stands. I agree with Hero's notion of taking a star off for a park that is not designated Off-Leash, because it's as much a pain for me to be attached to a leash as it is for Hero. I like fresh air, wildlife, and I also like big parks because I like the option of being able to go for a long walk. This influences the ratings in favour of the larger parks, so a short one star park might be very nice, it's just short, and you wouldn't want to drive across town for it.

How To Get There

The How to Get There sections give driving directions to the park or trailhead. If there are many ways of getting to a park, for instance if it is surrounded by roads, then that may be all the directions note. I tended to give more extensive directions if it is the kind of park for which people will drive across town. Small local walks will tend to have more basic instructions.

Sometimes there will be more than one How To Get There heading in a given park. There may be one set of directions for getting to the main part of the park and the parking lot and others for getting to trailheads that lead into the park. Sometimes there are many, many access points to a trail and I've had to pick one or two.

A good map of Greater Vancouver is essential to getting around, and is far too detailed for me to reproduce in this book. Get one. Use it!

Another thing that can be invaluable is a simple compass. There's just no substitute when you arrive at a junction of several paths and aren't sure which way to go. Get one. Use it!

Try and adopt the same attitude toward getting to the park as to the walk itself (see Zen and the Art of Dog Walking). Give yourself adequate time to get there, take it easy, and enjoy the scenery.

Trail Etiquette

One of the great things about owning a dog is that it makes you get out there, every day for most of us, and go for a walk. The health benefits of this are enormous for both you and your dog.

Most dogs need to go for a walk every day to stay happy and healthy. Hero gets either one long walk of more than one hour, or two short half-hour ones every day (OK, almost every day). How often and how far you walk your dog will be based on a complicated formula involving your dog's need for exercise, your own health and need for exercise, the time you have available in your busy schedule, the weather, and the availability of appropriate places to walk. I can help with the latter.

Many people don't want to bother driving even a short distance to walk their dog. Not that there's anything wrong with taking a nice jaunt around the neighbourhood if that's your pleasure, or if it's all you have time for, but I would like to suggest that putting some variety in where you walk can be very rewarding for both of you. Dogs and humans are intelligent creatures and are easily bored by repetition in their lives. Getting out to experience some new, or even less familiar sights (for the humans) and smells (for the dog) can be invigorating and motivate you to go for that walk when you might otherwise find it hard to make the effort. In almost all locations in the GVRD you will have a good number of walks within a 10-minute drive.

Leash Laws

The general rule in most GVRD municipalities is that dogs are supposed to be leashed at all times. The only time a dog is allowed off-leash is when on private property with the property owner's permission.

Walking your dog off-leash anywhere not designated for that activity can result in a fine. Recently more fines are being handed out as the Leash Wars heat up, especially in the more densely populated areas.

Currently there are very few parks in the GVRD where you can legally walk your dog off his leash. This book contains just over 40 locations so designated (see **Off-Leash Areas** in the index). Increasingly, however, there are more designated areas being set aside for this purpose by the more enlightened municipalities and the GVRD Parks Department.

Leashes and Reality

Dog owners have been practicing a kind of civil disobedience concerning their dogs ever since modern leash laws were introduced. It is an easily observable fact that most people ignore leash laws pretty well everywhere, probably because they recognize their dog's need to run as being worth the risk of a fine. Until recent times there were no Off-Leash Areas, so the choice was simple; obey the law and keep the poor dog on a leash its entire life, or ignore the law and allow the dog its freedom. I want to go on record here as being of the opinion that it is cruel and inhumane to keep an animal such as most dogs, which are built for speed, tethered to a much slower animal (humans) for its entire life. Dogs have been with humans longer than any other domestic animal; they are not going away. Therefore we must make provision for dogs in cities. We now have a few Off-Leash Areas, but not nearly enough.

On the other side of the coin, however, is the very real threat that some dogs, or dogs in general, can be to people, livestock, wildlife, and health concerns. If we as dog owners show we can be responsible when it counts then we may achieve the liberties we and our dogs desire. Be sensitive to areas of extreme ecological importance, keep your dog in sight at all times, keep him from harassing wildlife, livestock, as well as people, especially the very young and old, and tourists, some of whom are from countries where dogs are rare or wild.

Now, readers of this book would, of course, never willingly break the law by allowing their dogs off-leash where they're not supposed to be...but if they did...they would do it in areas where they will cause little or no impact, make very sure that their dogs behave exceptionally well, stay out of people's way and keep them in control at all times.

I will try and warn readers of parks where it is inadvisable to flaunt the leash laws, but common sense will serve you best.

Being Off-Leash

There's nothing worse than the sight of a dog with "owner malfunction." The dog isn't being "bad," it's just being a dog, happily greeting people in the special ways dogs have; a nose in the crotch, a nice wet kiss, jumping up on kids and old ladies, investigating interesting smells like picnics, and generally charging around with abandon. The human is to blame for any problems this causes, as we can't expect the dog to know better.

Whenever your dog is off-leash, whether in a designated Off-Leash Area or not, it is incumbent on you, the dog's handler, to remain in control of the dog at all times. That means the dog must stay **in sight** where you can control it, making very sure that it doesn't bother children or other dogs or people or livestock or wild animals or get into stuff it's not supposed to. If they go around a bend in the trail then you can't tell what they are encountering, now can you?

When approaching other dogs on the trail that are on-leash when your dog is off, regardless of whether or not the area you are in is designated as an Off-Leash Area, it is always a good idea to ask the owner of a leashed dog; "Is it friendly?" "Is it OK for them to meet?" Many dogs on-leash are there for a good reason; maybe they are new to the owner or maybe they're one of those dogs that just likes to take off, or maybe they don't socialize with other dogs very well. Don't let your dog wander into a conflict that may injure either or both dogs, or even you and the other owner.

Also give some thought to how urban the area is that you are walking in. You might be used to being able to get away with taking your dog off the leash in the wilds, but should think twice about it when you go to downtown parks.

When you approach people, especially small children, heel the dog and keep it away until you ascertain whether they would like to meet your dog or not. Telling a wary child, "He's friendly," can turn a worried frown into a smile and glean some welcome attention for your dog.

Dog Body Language

Hero asked me to include this brief note on body language, as he is often misunderstood by humans as well as by dogs that grew up mainly with humans. Hero grew up with seven other dogs, and he learned dog body language as opposed to human body language.

When a dog approaches another dog crouched low, it is lowering its profile to appear less threatening. It is not stalking the other dog. Hero does this, because he wants other dogs to know that he's just big and not aggressive.

A dog that is aggressive will stand on its toes with straight front legs and its head high. It will also raise its tail as high as it can and curl it over its back (provided it has that kind of tail) sometimes with a sharp bend near the top. It wants to look as big as possible. Aggressive dogs will often butt their chests up against each other in order to measure up the competition. Watch the tails; if they don't start wagging within a few seconds, it is best to call your dog away before they get more aggressive and start a fight.

Canine Good Citizen Program

A company in Coquitlam is running what they call the Canine Good Citizen Certification. The idea behind this certification is to demonstrate not only that your dog is obedient, as with standard obedience trials, but that it is good natured and able to mingle closely with humans and other dogs. Your dog must demonstrate that it can meet and interact with strange humans and other dogs in a friendly fashion, as well as obey a few basic commands geared toward showing that the dog is able to socialize in a controlled manner.

You can contact these people at: Human Dog Leadership Inc., 818 Millar Avenue, Coquitlam, BC, V3J 4K6, Tel: (604) 939-0803, Fax: (604) 939-0813

It is my hope that this program will be expanded and its status increased to allow dogs who pass the certification greater freedom from leashes. To me this is the way to regulate dogs. Let the good dogs (and owners) show that they can be responsible and have the freedom they deserve. Let the bad dogs (and owners) be controlled by leash laws if they will not or cannot control themselves.

Scatology

We all hate to pick up dog poop, but we also hate stepping in it and it's one of those things we have to do in order that the entire non-dog-owning world does not unite against us and ban us from parks entirely. I used to think that maybe sweeping it off the trail was OK, until I watched a family with little kids on a trail. Parents, do the kids actually walk on the trail? No, of course not. The kids were not on the trail, they were climbing around in the bushes next to the trail; sliding down banks and climbing back up the other side on all fours. Picking up your dog's excrement is not only polite, it's the only way of keeping our trails sanitary, and it's the law. JUST DO IT.

For when the dog has to go miles from anywhere, I have developed a kit for dog poop consisting of a light plastic bag, like a sandwich bag, to wrap around my hand and pick up the poop; a heavy ziplock bag, to seal it away from anything we are going to have to touch or clean; and a Tupperware™ container (clearly marked so that I don't ever mix it up with my food Tupperware) to keep the poop from stinking up my pack. Even on a hot day this keeps the poop away from us and our things, although you will want to store your lunch in another place, because, amazingly, the stink can still get through all those layers.

Now, what to do with the poop which you have so conscientiously picked up? As most of you will know, the law says that you are not allowed to put poop in a trash can, nor otherwise convey it to the landfill. What the sanitation department would like you to do is take it home and flush it down the toilet. Then, I suppose, you may dispose of the (comparatively) clean plastic bag in the garbage. This is an incredibly disgusting operation and I don't think many people actually do this. You can bury it in your back yard, if you have one, and you can even buy poop composters from pet stores, but this still leaves you holding the bag, as it were.

Fortunately, more and more enlightened municipalities and parks boards are putting garbage receptacles in advantageous places for dog walkers and their refuse. Even here, however, there are mixed messages. As mentioned above, excrement is not allowed in the landfill. I have called several garbage collection agencies around town and they seem to be as confused about the subject as the rest of us. I can only surmise, however, that when a garbage can is chained to a post bearing a sign admonishing you to scoop your poop, that the trash can is designated to receive said poop. I also bet that most people will agree that it is better there than on the trail.

Trail Wisdom

While most of the hikes in this book are relatively tame, some of them take you into the wilderness areas of Greater Vancouver. If you have never done any wilderness hiking, please read this next part and take its advice. Check out the section on what gear you need to take with you. Please note that this book does not claim to supply anything more than just a real basic primer on outdoorsmanship. Be careful to gauge your excursions to your ability.

The unpopulated areas around Vancouver, especially the mountains on the North Shore, go on for many miles without any kind of civilization–just trees, rocks, creeks, and animals. Weather can change in an hour here on the West Coast, so be prepared for a nice blue sky to turn into a chilling downpour. Make sure that you leave adequate time to return safely before nightfall. Take a change of clothing and always wear or carry something waterproof. Cheap plastic ponchos don't weigh much and can literally save your life.

Never hike into remote areas alone, and your four-legged friend does not count as another person. Even the collies who played Lassie on TV would be unlikely to run and get help for you should you fall and twist your ankle. More likely they would stay by you, which might keep you warm, unless they themselves were soaked, of course, in which case they would share their cold wet fur with you.

Write down your intended hike and leave it with a friend or with an attendant at the trailhead, or even just tell someone where you are going, and when you expect to be back. Tell them that, yes, they should worry if you don't contact them by such and such a time. Some trails, like Lynn Headwaters, actually have boxes where you can complete and leave a note saying when you left on your hike. Then, in the event you do not return, the park rangers can start looking for you.

Clothing

Having a Gore-Tex™ or other water-resistant or waterproof jacket, and possibly even water-resistant pants, is invaluable. The Lower Mainland is in a temperate rain forest. It rains a lot here, which we like; it makes the place green and lush. The very best place to be on a rainy day is in the woods. The canopy keeps some of the rain off, and the forest is truly beautiful in a murky sort of way. It may be an acquired taste, but Hero and I love it.

I would strongly advise that you get a pair of good hiking boots or waterproof runner/walkers. Waterproof is the most important part of this equation. As long as your feet are dry you can slog through any kind of rain, puddles, streams, mud, or snow to your destination.

Wear a hat, or at least carry one in your pack or have a hood on your jacket. An exposed head will drain your body's heat faster than you can imagine. A head exposed to the sun will cause you to overheat in much the same fashion.

Wear enough clothing to keep warm when you are active, then carry another warm thing to put on in case you are hurt and need to stay still. The synthetic material commonly known as Arctic fleece is ideal, as it is warm and water resistant and light.

Gear

Below is a list of things that you would be wise to carry on the wilder hikes in this book. It assumes that you have a day-pack in which to put them.

Compass

Waterproof plastic poncho

Space blanket

Flashlight

Food (for you and your dog!)

Change of clothing

Water or a water treatment method (drinking creek water can be hazardous)

Sun protection–sunglasses, sunscreen, hat

Pocket knife

Signaling whistle (for attracting the attention of rescuers)

Waterproof matches or a lighter, candles or fire starter

       (Ever tried to light a fire in a downpour, with wet wood?)

First Aid Kits for you and your dog (see below)

First Aid For Humans

Always carry a first aid kit. Even if it is just some Band-Aids, some antiseptic cream, and a tensor bandage, it can really help when you get bitten, stung, fall down, or twist your ankle. When you go further into the bush or up into the mountains you should carry a more extensive kit, as well as a few basic survival items. Your local hiking store will carry a range of these. For more extensive kits see your local St. John's Ambulance.

First Aid For Dogs

Probably the most frequent kind of injury you will encounter with your dog is a cut from sharp rocks or broken glass. Dogs are hard to give first aid to. You can't use a Band-Aid for a cut, and they hate having any kind of bandage on.

Your primary concern with cuts is to stop the bleeding. For this a salve (like calendula ointment) or petroleum jelly can aid in stopping the flow of blood. For really bad bleeds, putting pressure on the wound with a cloth bandage can help stop the flow of blood.

Cuts should be cleaned of any dirt and debris, and washed with soap (anti-bacterial hand soap is good) and water as soon as possible. If the cut is deep enough, you may want to take your dog to the vet and have it sutured.

An old sock, a plastic bag, and a few good elastic bands can be very useful for creating a temporary over-bandage. Be careful not to cut off circulation to the paw, however. Check for extremities becoming cold or swelling, both signs of circulation loss. A tensor bandage can wrap up a sprained paw on a dog just like a sprained ankle on a human. You will most likely want to have a vet make sure there are no broken bones.

In the days that follow, watch for any redness or swelling that may indicate infection. Sniff the wound. Infection smells bad.

If your dog has been bitten by a wild animal, it probably needs a rabies shot. You should also check your dog and yourself for ticks after walks in the woods or tall grass.

About Rivers

Some hikes in this book have a WARNING entry about the rivers you will be hiking next to. You will occasionally see signs on trails telling you that the cliffs are dangerous, and that you should keep back. Obey these signs. Every year people don't and lose their lives. In large rivers such as the Seymour and the Capilano in North Vancouver the current can be incredibly strong. Be extremely cautious at any time when venturing into such a river. If it is in flood, keep your dog away from the banks. If your dog is swept away by the current, remember that it is generally a much stronger swimmer than people, and the best thing that you can do is run along the bank, call and encourage it, and be there to help your dog out if it is able to make it back to shore.

If You Become Lost

Don't Panic! Easier said than done, but try to keep a clear head. If you have a pack with a few survival items in it you should be fine.

Stay where you are. People who are lost usually wander further away from the trail rather than getting back to it.

Build or seek shelter. Stay as warm and dry as you can. Protect yourself from sun and wind.

Be visible–light a fire, lay out bright clothing you don't need. Be audible–blow a whistle, shout–so that rescuers can find you.

Naturally people will come looking for you because you told someone where you were going and they have missed you by now. Right?

Plants

"Take nothing but memories, leave nothing but footprints."

Most of the parks in this book have many people walking through them every day. The flower that you pick which wilts in the car on the way home might last several days left in the woods and be enjoyed by literally hundreds of people. Same goes for the plants your dog digs up.

Also, flowers are reproductive organs for plants and picking them will lessen the number of flowers in succeeding years. In many parks picking flowers or any plant is illegal.

Wildlife

One can encounter many forms of wildlife on the GVRD's trails, including the Pacific Giant Salamander, that apparently barks, and, one of the most spectacular, the Giant Banana Slug, that doesn't bark.

When dealing with any form of wildlife, whether it's something you can crush by stepping on it or something that can crush you just as easily, the key word has to be **respect**.

Raccoons, deer, coyotes, skunks, squirrels, and a variety of birds of course, are all common in the Lower Mainland. Bears and cougars are not uncommon. Up in the Fraser Valley I have also seen possum and even porcupines. It is completely unacceptable to let your dog harass these animals. Possum, squirrels, grouse, and deer have no defense against dogs, while raccoons, coyotes, bears, cougars, and porcupines can injure or even kill your dog. You know what skunk encounters do. Keep your dog in sight. Call them off if they chase things. Likewise, humans, leave wild animals alone. Wild animals, even a squirrel, will bite you if you get close enough. Don't feed them. Don't touch them. Raccoons are cuddly looking, but they can be extremely savage. The one exception here might be the Whiskey Jack or Grey Jay, which is a very friendly bird who inhabits the mountainous areas and who will steal your lunch or eat right out of your hand.

For the most part, however, animals will leave you alone. We'll deal here with stuff you should know about a couple of species that might not.

Coyotes

I have heard tales that coyotes will play with dogs, entice them into the woods, and then kill them. I am not sure if these tales are true, but I do know that they will fight with dogs and even eat smaller dogs. Coyotes are a good reason to keep your dog in sight and under control at all times. If your dog is off in the bush you have no idea what it is meeting in there.

Coyotes are creatures indigenous to this area and have at least as much right to be here as we and our dogs do. Respect them, leave them alone and hope that they do the same for you and your dog.

Bears

The kind of bears you are most likely to encounter in Greater Vancouver are black bears, as opposed to grizzly bears, which are much larger and more aggressive. This is not to say that black bears (who can be over 270 kg.) are not to be treated with the utmost respect. They are aggressive animals who can be extremely dangerous. Bears can run as fast as a racehorse, they are strong swimmers, and they can climb trees. They have good eyesight and hearing, and an acute sense of smell. Black bears can be black, brown, cinnamon, or blond. Bears can be found year-round in all parks, even those near urban centres.

If you encounter a bear, talk to it in a friendly tone of voice and back slowly away. Show it that you are not aggressive, but don't run away. You don't want to provoke the bear into a fight or flight reaction, nor do you want to make it think of you as prey. Watch out for cubs and don't get between them and their mother. Obviously you need to keep your dog away and as calm as possible during all of this.

Make noise as you travel and bears will generally avoid you. If a black bear attacks, the general consensus is that you should roll into a ball, with your back to the bear and your hands over the back of your neck. If the attack persists then you should try and fight it off–as a human being you will probably want to employ some kind of tool, like a pointed stick. Playing dead is not appropriate with black bears.

Cougars

Cougars (also known as mountain lions) are very dangerous animals. Though they seldom attack humans, they are predators who would look upon a small dog as a viable meal and a large dog as a threat. Keep your dog in sight at all times. Do not allow it to chase a cougar if you do encounter one. A stout walking staff is probably your best defense, but keeping out of their way is better.

If you do encounter a cougar, however, talk confidently and calmly to it. Move slowly away, but do not turn your back to it. If it threatens, yell and wave your arms, try and make it see you as a threat, not a meal. If it attacks, fight back with anything you can lay your hands on. Many people have survived cougar attacks this way.

Make noise as you travel and cougars will generally avoid you. If you find cougar cubs, leave the area immediately. Cougars bury half-eaten meals for later, so if you find a half-eaten carcass, leave the area immediately.

In my travels I have never seen a cougar inside the GVRD and in all likelihood you will never encounter one of these beautiful but dangerous creatures.

Zen and the Art of Dog Walking

Now that we've gone through the how to's and the what if's and the do's and don'ts, a word about what we're all after; exercise for ourselves and our canine friends, and the peace of mind and tranquillity that comes through getting out into the Great Outdoors, even if it's just a small oasis surrounded by development.

Try to be mindful of the activity you are involved in. Focus on the moment. Give yourself a break and try and stop yourself from dwelling on your problems. Don't barrel through your walk as if to get to the end of the hike is the only objective. Stop when your dog wants to investigate something, and while you allow it the time to enjoy itself, remember to enjoy yourself too. Notice the particular beauty of any plants or rocks nearby. Breathe deeply. Look at the view. Watch your dog as it exhibits that happy exuberance that dogs excel at. Enjoy.

The Trails

All trails have been arranged alphabetically within municipalities, which are also arranged alphabetically. Sometimes I have grouped smaller municipalities with their larger neighbour. To anyone with strong municipal allegiances, I apologize for this.

When deciding on whether a trail is right for you, note the time it takes to do a walk, the difficulty rating, and the overall rating we have given it.

Our "Paws and Stars" rating system gives you an idea of whether a park or trail is suitable for an outing or more for just everyday use. Generally speaking, the higher the rating, the more it is worth some effort to get to a particular park.

Burnaby

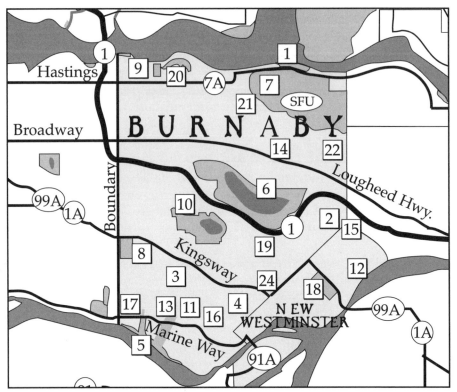

Looking west from Burnaby Mountain.

Burnaby

(Including New Westminster)

Burnaby has an abundance of parks including Burnaby Mountain, a couple of large lakes; Deer Lake and Burnaby Lake, some parks which line the shore of both Burrard Inlet and the Fraser, and a number of ravine parks on the south side. New Westminster, being one of the older and more developed parts of the GVRD, has few parks suitable for dog walking, but is close to many of the best Burnaby Parks.

Barnet Marine Park

Park Number	1	Fishing	
Trail Difficulty	1	Swimming	Drinking
Trail Condition	Excellent to good	Access Washroom	Water Prohibited
Time	30 minutes		

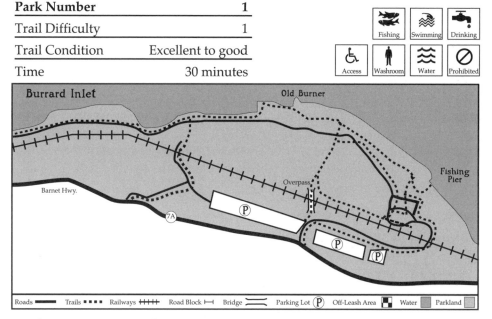

As the name suggests, this park borders on Burrard Inlet. Dogs are not allowed in the main part of this park which is dotted with picnic tables. To the west of the pedestrian overpass is a wide flat trail which runs along the shore. This deteriorates into an old road which is still quite passable. There are a few tiny beaches along the way, quite private in the colder times.

This park was the site of an old mill and the remains of the scrap burner make a kind of little pier which you can walk out on. Kids will love this, and it's about as close to ancient ruins as you get in this town. Kinda noisy due to the presence of the gun club just above the highway, but nice view of Burrard Inlet.

Water quality in Burrard Inlet is Fair.

How To Get There

Take the Barnet Highway, either from the east end of Hastings Street or from Port Moody. At the gun club, turn north toward the water (there are park signs on the water side). Park in the first parking lot (to your left) and either walk over the pedestrian walkway or down the road which leads from the west of the parking lot.

Hero's Rating: 🐾 🐾 🐾   Human's Rating: ★ ★ ★

Brunette River

Park Number	2
Trail Difficulty	1
Trail Condition	Excellent
Time	30 minutes

The trail is a service road that follows the river from very near **Burnaby Lake** to North Road. The Brunette here is a medium-sized shallow river. The walk is treed on either side. Good place to see waterfowl and herons.

Water quality in Brunette River is Good.

How To Get There

From the Lougheed or Trans-Canada Highway (#1) take the Cariboo exit to Gaglardi Way (exit #37 on the Trans-Canada). Get onto Cariboo Road, where it goes west of Gaglardi. Turn right on Cariboo Place. Park before the turnaround.

Or access on the west side of North Road by **Hume Park**.

Hero's Rating: 🐾 🐾   Human's Rating: ★ ★

BC Parkway and Highland Park Line

Park Number	3
Trail Difficulty	1
Trail Condition	Excellent
Time	Various

This trail basically follows the Skytrain route, and is part of a linear, 19-km park strip that connects Westminster Quay to False Creek. Fabulous if you want to walk or cycle through any of these areas. Lousy if you want a nice walk with your dog. To be honest, I did not walk the whole thing; Hero just found it too obnoxious. There are several parks along the way, such as **Central Park**. Although some sections are nicer, such as the bit just south of Rumble by Edmonds where the track turns down toward New Westminster, (due to become condos and the 10th Avenue extension), most of the time there is a busy road paralleling the trail.

How To Get There
Can be accessed throughout Burnaby along the Skytrain route, including in **Central Park**.

Hero's Rating: No Paws   **Human's Rating: ★**

Byrne Creek Ravine Park

Byrne Creek Ravine Park is a wild treed ravine with trails on either side. Ron McLean Park lies just to the north.

Byrne Creek Trail

Park Number	4
Trail Difficulty	1 - 2
Trail Condition	Excellent
Time	30 minutes

Ron McLean Park is a grassy park with a playground, washrooms, and tennis courts, and it lies just north of several trails that run north-south through Byrne Creek Ravine Park, which is a wild treed ravine with trails on either side.

The trail skirts the west edge of the park by the road, then cuts across to Marine Way and Southpoint. About halfway down there is a long staircase taking you into the ravine where water access is easy. The creek is fairly clean.

How To Get There
Take Rumble to Hedley, then south on Hedley, which turns into a lane and bears to the right. There is a parking lot by some tennis courts. The trailhead is to the west of the courts.

Hero's Rating: 🐾 🐾   **Human's Rating: ★ ★**

East Side Trails

Park Number	4
Trail Difficulty	1 - 2
Trail Condition	Rustic
Time	30 minutes

The east side of the creek is accessible from the main part of Ron McLean park and contains a wide variety of trails. There is a great deal of development going on there at present, however, and many of the trailheads are being lost. One trail follows the ridge of the ravine most of the way down, not quite reaching Marine Drive, which is a pity because it would make a great loop trail if it hooked up with the **Byrne Creek Trail**.

How To Get There

To get to Ron McLean park, take Rumble to Hedley, then south on Hedley. There is a parking lot here.

Hero's Rating: 🐾   **Human's Rating:** ★ ★

Paved Way

Park Number	4
Trail Difficulty	1
Trail Condition	Excellent
Time	15 minutes

There is this wonderful paved walkway which follows the eastern edge of the park. Wonderful especially if you come upon it rather suddenly like I did; a wide paved road in the middle of the woods with street lamps all along it, or if you are like the young lady in the wheelchair I met there, cruising with another lady and their dog.

How To Get There

This walkway can be accessed from inside the park or from the **BC Parkway**. There is also a branch of it that threads over through some apartment buildings to the old dump which is also the site of the future Taylor Park.

Hero's Rating: 🐾   **Human's Rating:** ★ ★

Ron McLean Park

Park Number	4
Trail Difficulty	n/a
Trail Condition	n/a
Time	n/a

Ron McLean Park is a grassy park with a playground, washrooms, and tennis courts, and it lies just north of Byrne Creek Ravine Park.

Hero's Rating: No Paws   **Human's Rating: No stars**

Burnaby Fraser Foreshore Park

Park Number	5
Trail Difficulty	1
Trail Condition	Good
Time	3 - 4 hours

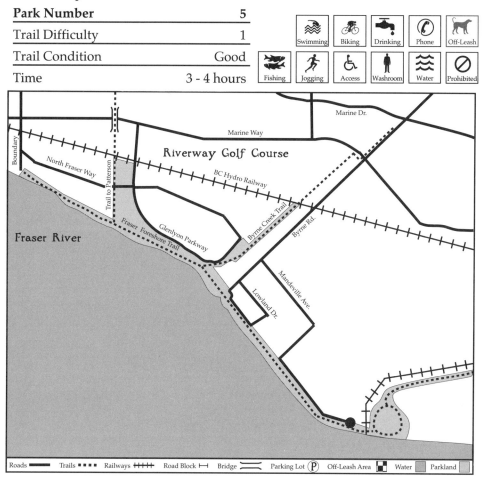

A thin strip of a park which hugs the Fraser River. The main trail follows the river and two others follow sloughs north. Some maps posted in the park would have you believe that they form a square with another trail so you can circle back, but the only way I could find to connect the north ends of the two trails that run that way is to walk along the railway tracks. My mother told me this is a dangerous thing to do and I can't recommend it, especially with a dog.

Water quality in the Fraser River North Arm is Fair.

How To Get There
From Marine Way go to the south end of Byrne to access the main park entrance and the Fraser Foreshore Trail.

The Fraser Foreshore Trail

Park Number	5
Trail Difficulty	1
Trail Condition	Good
Time	30 minutes - 2 hours

The main trail follows the riverbank and runs about 3 km in three parts; from Boundary east to the first branching trailhead that runs north, from there to the main picnic area and parking lot, and from the main area east. Think of each 1-km chunk as being a half hour to walk through and back again.

The most westerly part of the Fraser Foreshore trail is a proposed Off-Leash Area. At the time of this writing you still need to have your dog on a leash, but there is signage alluding to the possibility of such zoning in the future. Watch for updated signage. Unfortunately this part of the trail runs right beside several parking lots and a cafe with picnic tables on the grass. Both dog off-leash hazards. Access to the river is not bad at the western end of this section of the trail, but gets quite mucky before turning to sand in the following section.

The middle part of the trail is probably the nicest, although construction was evident to the north, I believe it is the golf course expanding. A corridor of alder and cottonwood line the shore.

The eastern part of the trail is more developed, less wooded, and ends up running along the street.

Just past the official end of these trails (the Burnaby Correctional Facility for Women appears on your left) you can walk along an old access road into a park which is under development. Burnaby Parks is planning on putting in a meadow there. As a dog walk, this provided a little more open space, but not as great access to the water.

How To Get There

You can access the Off-Leash Area at the south end of Boundary. The other parts of this trail can be accessed at the main park entrance at the south end of Byrne.

Hero's Rating: 🐾 🐾 🐾   Human's Rating: ★ ★ ★

Byrne Creek Trail

Park Number	5
Trail Difficulty	1
Trail Condition	Good
Time	45 minutes

There are actually trails on both sides of the "creek," which is more what I would call a canal or a slough; mucky, slow-moving, and clogged with bulrush and cattails. The western trail ends at the golf course, and the eastern trail terminates almost at Marine Way. There are plans to improve this trailhead. You have to cross the tracks and a road. There is development and commercial/industrial property next to the trail. Nevertheless I saw a turtle in the slough, a rare sight in any part of the GVRD.

How To Get There

From Marine Way go to the south end of Byrne to access this trail at the main park entrance.

Hero's Rating: 🐾 🐾   **Human's Rating:** ★ ★

The Trail up to Patterson

Park Number	5
Trail Difficulty	1
Trail Condition	Good
Time	45 minutes

I am loathe to give this trail a name since no one else has, so The Trail up to Patterson will have to suffice. It runs north from between the first and second sections of the trail, eventually crossing Marine Way on an overpass and ending at the south end of Patterson on Marine Drive. You have to cross the tracks and a road. Interesting to note, the intersection of this trail and the train tracks smells like hot buttered popcorn.

The trail on the other side of the overpass was nothing special, but the field just past the overpass had some curious cows in it the day we were there, and they came over to say hi, which Hero enjoyed enormously. There was a hedge separating them from us, which was probably a good thing.

How To Get There

Access in park or on Marine Drive and Patterson.

Hero's Rating: 🐾 🐾   **Human's Rating:** ★ ★

Burnaby Lake Regional Park

Park Number	6
Trail Difficulty	1
Trail Condition	Good
Time	2 hours

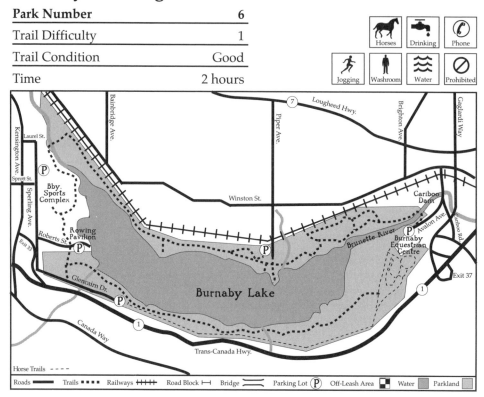

This park contains a young forest around a sizable lake. Staying off the horse trails, there is just one trail, with a few minor extra loops, which circumnavigates the lake. The trail is wide and raised and made of wood chips, very springy, and joggers love it. Bessie loves to roll in the wood chips. They do not, however, take very kindly to people flaunting the leash laws, especially on the weekend when it is crowded. There are lots of little creeks going in and out of the lake, and therefore lots of mud.

The highway is a bit noisy on the south side, but the lake is beautiful; full of lily pads and waterfowl. Make sure your dog doesn't disturb the latter. You can even go canoeing here, or just watch the rowers from the rowing club.

Water quality in Burnaby Lake is Fair.

How To Get There

Piper Avenue Entrance: From the Lougheed Highway, turn south onto Brighton Avenue, which is west of Gaglardi and east of Kensington. Turn east onto Winston Street. Turn south onto Piper Avenue.

Cariboo Dam Entrance: From the Lougheed Highway, turn south onto Brighton Avenue, which is west of Gaglardi and east of Kensington. Turn east onto Winston Street. Turn south onto Cariboo Road. Turn west onto Avalon Avenue at the Equestrian Centre sign.

Glencairn Trailhead Entrance: From the Lougheed, take the Kensington exit south, then immediately get into the left lane. From the first left turn lane, turn east onto Laurel Street and then south onto Sperling Avenue. Sperling turns into Glencairn Drive. Watch for park signs.

Hero's Rating: 🐾 🐾 🐾   **Human's Rating:** ★ ★ ★

Burnaby Mountain Park and Conservation Area

Park Number	7
Trail Difficulty	2 - 4
Trail Condition	Good
Time	up to 3 or 4 hours

Biking | Drinking | Phone
Jogging | Washroom | Water | Prohibited

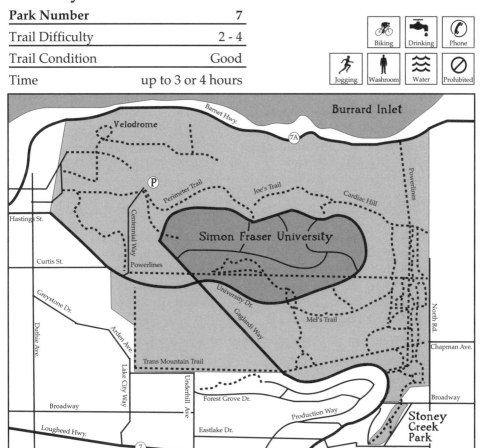

The park occupies one corner of the Burnaby Mountain Conservation Area, and contains Horizons Restaurant, a rose garden, and the Harry Jerome Sports Centre; a velodrome, which is a track for racing bicycles. For our purposes I will deal mainly with the Conservation Area, in which there are many trails. The main trail starts at Burnaby Mountain Park and, heading east, connects to a number of linking trails, Perimeter Trail, Joe's Trail, the aptly named Cardiac Hill, and Mel's Trail, which together circumnavigate the university. These trails slope toward the east and look out through dense foliage, mainly maples and alder, to Burrard Inlet.

On the east side of the park there is a complicated network of trails and powerlines. If you follow any of these toward Burrard Inlet, they end suddenly, sometimes with Do Not Enter signs on the trail and sometimes they just run into the Barnet Highway. The water icon, therefore, refers to a number of small creeks.

Following Mel's Trail from where it meets Cardiac Hill, it heads south, then west, climbing up to meet the powerlines. Watch for Gaglardi Way, which you must cross.

As a side route, you can drop down a very steep trail and then hike back up the **Trans Mountain Trail**. This is a wide access road, for the most part, which starts at the corner of Arden Avenue and Shellmont Street, crosses Gaglardi Way, and continues through the park to Chapman Avenue on the east border.

There are two sets of Powerline Trails running almost together. The lower one seems to peter out into blackberry bushes, but if one has faith and does not doubt their fearless trail leader, one will find that they do join up and cross Centennial Way as the map says. Follow Centennial Way back up to the parking lot, or dip down into the velodrome part of the park if you have the time.

How To Get There
Take Hastings Street east to just before it turns into the Barnet Highway (just past Sperling). Follow the signs to SFU. The right-hand lane goes past the concrete statue shop and continues up the hill toward Simon Fraser University. Watch for signage directing you to the park or you will end up at the university. There is a turnoff on your left to Centennial Way. Signs in the parking lot tell you "patrons only." This means patrons of the park (yes, that's you) not just of the acclaimed Horizons Restaurant.

You can also access this park through Stoney Creek Park, or via the Trans Mountain Trail mentioned above, at the corner of Arden Avenue and Shellmont Street.

Hero's Rating: 🐾 🐾   **Human's Rating:** ★ ★ ★

Central Park

Park Number	8
Trail Difficulty	1
Trail Condition	Excellent
Time	up to 1 hour

Central Park is a busy urban park with children's playgrounds, a sports complex, a running track, tennis courts, an outdoor pool, pitch and putt, and a horseshoe pitch, as well as a couple of ponds, all of which are off-limits to dogs.

There are a few short trails, all very well groomed and used. Very busy park. Definitely not the place to flaunt leash laws. A bit too urban for Hero's tastes. Pretty nice woods, but just in tiny little clumps.

How To Get There

Central Park is at Kingsway and Boundary. Access off Boundary, Imperial Street, or Patterson Avenue.

Hero's Rating: 🐾   **Human's Rating:** ★

Confederation Park

Park Number	9
Trail Difficulty	2 - 3
Trail Condition	Excellent
Time	30 minutes

Confederation Park is in the middle of the **Scenic Trail System**. In the upper (southern) half you will find a number of amenities such as a fitness centre and spray pool. There is even a model railway you can ride, which is actually in the lower part of the park, right next to the trailhead.

The lower (northern) half of Confederation Park has been kept in its natural state. The main trail here is referred to as the Penzance Trail. It is in a heavily-wooded area on the side of the hill slopes down toward Burrard inlet. It is currently an Off-Leash Area on a one-year trial basis. The forest is mainly deciduous; maples and alder, and is fabulous in the fall.

How To Get There

Take Hastings to Willingdon, then go north on Willingdon. There is signage and a parking lot on Penzance Drive.

Hero's Rating: 🐾 🐾   **Human's Rating:** ★ ★

Deer Lake Park

Park Number	**10**
Trail Difficulty	1 - 2
Trail Condition	Excellent
Time	up to 2 hours

Biking | Drinking | Phone

Access | Washroom | Water | Prohibited

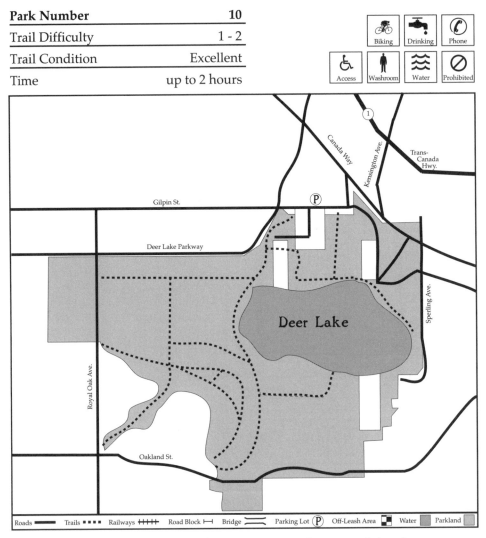

Roads ▬▬ Trails ▪▪▪▪ Railways ┼┼┼┼ Road Block ├─┤ Bridge ═ Parking Lot (P) Off-Leash Area ▪ Water ▪ Parkland ▪

As I said in the introduction to this book, doing the research has been an eye-opener in that many parks are bigger and better than I imagined they would be. Deer Lake Park is one of these.

I was only familiar with the portion of the park right off Canada Way; the Shadbolt Centre and the beach where you can rent canoes. Deer Lake Park also contains a small forest and large fields with tall grasses.

If you follow the shore trail to the west, it dips up around some private property and reenters the park in a nice deciduous forest. The path becomes a boardwalk which winds through a marsh. Those of you who habitually defy leash laws would do well to put the dog on this one time; as the many posted signs attest, this is a very rare bit of marshland that is vital for the continued existence of several species of birds and mammals.

The southwest end of the lake has several paths through the marsh and grassy fields, that I found lovely on the bright summer day we visited. It reminded me of how the country used to look around Vancouver when I was a kid (circa early 1960's). The land climbs to the southwest and there is a lookout there that you can mount. The paths all circle back for the most part and you could spend hours going in circles and cutting back if you wanted to cover them all. The park has maps posted at crossways with "you are here" pointers.

Water quality in Deer Lake is Fair.

How To Get There
Take the Trans-Canada Highway (#1) and get off on the Deer Lake/Kensington South exit (#33). Turn left (west) on Canada Way and follow the signs (you immediately turn right) to enter the park.

Hero's Rating: 🐾   **Human's Rating:** ★ ★ ★

Froggers Creek Ravine Park

Park Number	11
Trail Difficulty	1 - 3
Trail Condition	Good to rustic
Time	15 minutes

The park consists of a small grassy play field on a hill with some structures for kids to climb on (including one of those Buck Rogers-like space ships we used to love). There is a small trail down to the creek and a couple trails below the grassy field.

How To Get There
Access off SE Marine Drive east of Royal Oak.

Hero's Rating: 🐾   **Human's Rating:** ★

Glenbrook Ravine

Park Number	12
Trail Difficulty	2
Trail Condition	Good
Time	30 minutes

Fraserview Recreation Centre is at the bottom of this little trail, surrounded by young trees. We saw a coyote on this trail, just to let you know how prevalent they are.

How To Get There

Access is through the formal gardens behind the recreation centre (don't let your dog stomp the flower beds). Fraserview Recreation Centre is on Jamieson Court off Richmond Street just above Columbia in New Westminster.

Hero's Rating: 🐾   **Human's Rating:** ★

Gray Creek Ravine Park

Park Number	13
Trail Difficulty	2 - 3
Trail Condition	Poor
Time	15 minutes

Very poor overgrown trails.

How To Get There

Access off SE Marine Drive east of Royal Oak.

Hero's Rating: 🐾   **Human's Rating: No Stars**

Harold Wince Conservation Area

Park Number	14
Trail Difficulty	1 - 3
Trail Condition	Good to rustic
Time	30 minutes - 1 hour

This mainly consists of a broad grassy way under the powerlines. Paths also run from here through the woods up to the condos.

How To Get There

Access the powerlines at Broadway and Underhill or Broadway and Production Way.

Hero's Rating: 🐾   **Human's Rating:** ★

Hume Park

Park Number	15
Trail Difficulty	1 - 3
Trail Condition	Poor
Time	15 minutes

Hume Park has a children's playground and a grass playing field by the river. A very rough trail goes down the Brunette River to the east. Careful, it spills out onto train tracks.

How To Get There

Access off the east side of Columbia Street just south of the Trans-Canada Highway (#1).

Hero's Rating: 🐾   **Human's Rating:** ★

John Matthews Creek Ravine Park

Park Number	16
Trail Difficulty	2 - 3
Trail Condition	Rustic to poor
Time	10 minutes

The trails in this park are overgrown and hard to follow.

How To Get There

Access off SE Marine Drive east of Gilly.

Hero's Rating: 🐾   **Human's Rating: No Stars**

Kaymar Creek Ravine Park

Park Number	17
Trail Difficulty	1 - 3
Trail Condition	Good to rustic
Time	15 minutes

There is this lovely trail running up beside the creek, the bed of which has actually been cobbled at some point, probably long ago, and the water rushes over the cobble stones in a most pleasing way. On the west side of the park there is a deer trail you can follow if you are fairly intrepid.

How To Get There

Access off SE Marine Drive east of Patterson.

Hero's Rating: 🐾   **Human's Rating:** ★ ★

Queens Park

Park Number	18
Trail Difficulty	1
Trail Condition	Good
Time	30 minutes

Queens Park is an open grassy park with lots of trees and bushes. There are no real trails, but it goes for quite a distance down McBride Boulevard and could provide a decent walk. Take care around McBride as it is very busy.

How To Get There
Queens Park is a very open park and can be accessed from McBride Boulevard or 1st Street on the other side.

Hero's Rating: 🐾   **Human's Rating:** ★

Robert Burnaby Park

Park Number	19
Trail Difficulty	2
Trail Condition	Good
Time	30 minutes - 1 hour

A sizable forested park with sections of open field. All the trails slope down through the park from 4th Street to Hill Avenue, and generally to the north. The forest is mixed; cedars and maples and hemlocks.

The Off-Leash Area is due west of the Hill Avenue parking lot. It runs over to, and includes, the BC Hydro right-of-way (powerlines). The powerlines here run over a wide grassy swath, which is currently an Off-Leash Area on a one-year trial basis. Just a great place for dogs that love to run and chase. Just above the Off-Leash Area is a nice clear stream. Some of the creeks further up are a bit mucky.

How To Get There
From Canada Way, you can take a number of streets to get to the park. The way the city of Burnaby suggests is northeast along 16th, then left on 1st. You can access the Off-Leash Area at the bottom of Hill Avenue off Wedgewood, which is where 20th would be if there was one. The Off-Leash Area runs from here up to 4th, where there is another parking lot at Elwell. The park is adjacent to but not accessible from the Trans-Canada Highway (#1).

Hero's Rating: 🐾 🐾 🐾   **Human's Rating:** ★ ★ ★

Scenic Trail System

Park Number	20
Trail Difficulty	1 - 2
Trail Condition	Excellent
Time	1 - 2 hours

The Scenic Trail System is a series of parks, roads, and trails that run along the south side of Indian Arm, with **Confederation Park** right in the middle. You can walk the **Penzance Trail** and then head either west or east on the Scenic Trail System. Either way, you have to cross the road, and the trail is no longer Off-Leash once you leave **Confederation Park**, but the walk is quite nice, with views of the water and the far shore.

To the east you cross Penzance Road and walk through a forest of maples, eventually arriving in a residential area, and ending up on Hastings Street across from Kensington Park, where there is a pitch and putt.

To the west you walk through several playgrounds surrounded by a residential area before once again entering the forest at Montrose Park. The trail continues along a broad path, with many smaller paths leading down a steep bank toward the railroad tracks and eventually meets with tiny Bates Park just before the Second Narrows Bridge. I would advise against attempting to get down to or across the tracks.

How To Get There

Access at **Confederation Park** at the north end of Willingdon, and on Hastings Street just east of Fell Avenue, or at Montrose Park (some maps say Second Narrows Park) at the north end of Boundary, or McGill Park at the north end of Carleton.

Hero's Rating: 🐾   Human's Rating: ★ ★

Squint Lake Park

Park Number	21
Trail Difficulty	1
Trail Condition	Good
Time	30 minutes

The trail runs through a bit of bush that circles the park. It starts between the parking lot and the baseball diamond that it goes around. It then heads along the edge of the golf course until it reaches the point where Shellmont Street meets Arden. Across the street is an access point to the **Trans Mountain Trail**. You can go a little further, either along the paved walkway that lines the road, or along a deer trail that continues to skirt the golf course. Do not try to circumnavigate the golf course, you will end up walking on the road for a long, long way.

Hero thinks golfing is dumb, but then most golfers probably have an opinion about walking around with a stick in your mouth, so...

How To Get There
Take Hastings to Sperling, go south on Sperling, east on Curtis, south on Duthie, then east on Greystone. At the next intersection there are signs for the Stone's Throw Pub. Turn right here, then left into the park. Park in the first parking lot to your left. Dogs are not allowed on the golf course.

Hero's Rating: 🐾   **Human's Rating:** ★

Stoney Creek Park

Park Number	22
Trail Difficulty	1 - 3
Trail Condition	Excellent to poor
Time	15 minutes - 3 hours

This park has several trails, most of which end up in the **Burnaby Mountain** Conservation Area. The main trail is on the east bank of the creek and is well-maintained gravel, level and flat, and ends at North Road. Just a couple hundred paces before North Road, stepping stones take you into a woods where there are several winding, twisting deer trails (frequented by cyclists) that climb into the Conservation Area, and link with the **Trans Mountain Pipeline** and the powerlines there.

Most of the other trails in this park are rustic, and some can be very muddy. A trail goes down the west side, ending up at the train tracks and Government Street, almost, but not quite, connecting with the **Brunette River** trail. Trails also go upstream on the west side, just a block or so up to the school.

How To Get There
Take the Lougheed Highway (#7), turn north on Production Way, then east on Eastlake, which more or less becomes Beaverbrook Drive. You can access this park at the corner of Beaverbrook Drive and Beaverbrook Crescent.

Hero's Rating: 🐾 🐾 🐾   **Human's Rating:** ★ ★

Coquitlam

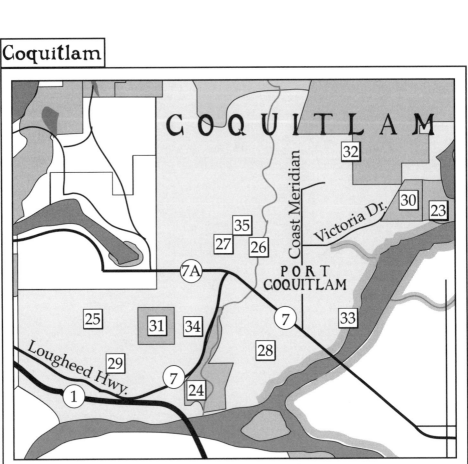

View from High Knoll in Minnekhada Regional Park.

Coquitlam
(Including Port Coquitlam)

Coquitlam has a few ravine parks on its upper slopes, including the Coquitlam River. Mundy Park and Colony Farm Regional Park are sizable parks in this municipality. Port Coquitlam has the varied and extensive PoCo Trail which includes many miles of dyke walks on the Pitt River. Minnekhada Park is a bit more rustic, and Burke Mountain, located just a little further up, becomes true wilderness.

Addington Marsh

Park Number	23
Trail Difficulty	1
Trail Condition	Poor
Time	3 hours

Water

The **Pitt-Addington Marsh Wildlife Management Area** refers to a vast reserve on both sides of the Pitt River. Look under **Grant Narrows Regional Park** in the **Outlying Areas** section of this book for information about the Pitt Meadows side of this reserve. On the PoCo side there is a dyke that circles about 200 hectares of marshland situated adjacent to **Minnekhada Regional Park** (see under this heading for a map of both parks). Dog walkers must be very conscious of the fact that this area contains very sensitive nesting sites and a variety of wildlife such as beaver, who could easily be disturbed by a dog.

The trail encircles the park, skirting the foothills on the west side and walking the dyke between the marsh and the Pitt River on the other four sides. Not your average dyke walk; the trail is extremely overgrown, which was kinda fun and kinda hard to walk through. Walking through the tall grasses was fun, but our legs got soaked. Waterproof pants do not happen to be the answer in this case, as they would be thoroughly shredded by the brambles. Wear tough pants you don't care about, and waterproof hiking boots. I don't think Hero and Bessie much liked being hemmed in by the tall grass for that length of time. But there is river access. The marsh is very beautiful, home to many birds and beaver. There is a nice view up the valley and a couple of lookout platforms.

Water Quality in the Pitt River is Good, so I would assume the same for the marsh.

How To Get There
Access this park from the Lodge parking lot at **Minnekhada Regional Park**. From the Lougheed Highway, turn north on Coast Meridian Road. Two and a

half km along this road turn right onto Apel Drive. Follow the signs to the park entrance. Cedar Drive takes you to Oliver Road which will take you to the Lodge Parking Lot.

Take the Fern Trail or walk along Oliver Road. This will get you to the south end of the marsh and take you around in a counterclockwise direction. If you go the other way, you get to do your climbing over the foothills first and circle the marsh later.

Hero's Rating: 🐾 🐾   **Human's Rating:** ★ ★ ★

Burke Mountain
(See Pinecone Burke Provincial Park)

Colony Farm Regional Park

Park Number	24
Trail Difficulty	1
Trail Condition	Excellent
Time	up to 5 - 6 hours

Marshy grassland with gravel roads and canal-like waters. There are two parts to this park, divided by the Coquitlam River. The GVRD apparently plans to install a bridge to replace the one that some creeps burned down, but until this happens, you have to visit each half separately.

Water quality in the Coquitlam River is Fair.

Eastern Half

Park Number	24
Trail Difficulty	1
Trail Condition	Excellent
Time	2 - 3 hours

The main road leads down a dyke through marshy woods to a T in the road where the woods end and true marshland begins. The left-hand branch terminates near Mary Hill Road. Hawks and other birds abound here. Watch that your dog does not disturb nesting birds. The right branch circles down to the Mary Hill Bypass, where it also splits, the left half again terminating at Mary Hill Road and the right half going under the bridge and then along the Mary Hill Bypass.

How To Get There
Get to the section of the Lougheed Highway (#7) that runs north-south between the Trans-Canada Highway (#1) and where the Lougheed Highway and the

Barnet Highway (#7A) meet. (Take exit #44, just before the Port Mann Bridge).

To access the Eastern section of the park, take the Pitt River Road going east. This intersection is right by **Riverview** Hospital and has the distinctive GVRD green with yellow lettering signage. Immediately you will go over a bridge crossing the Coquitlam River. There is a parking lot on the north side of Pitt River Road. You can walk under the bridge and along a trail which will take you to the main road going into the park.

Hero's Rating: 🐾 🐾 🐾   **Human's Rating: ★ ★ ★**

Western Half

Park Number	24
Trail Difficulty	1
Trail Condition	Good to Poor
Time	2 hours

Similar to the Eastern Half but a little wilder. There is a trail that follows the river which is very muddy. The river here is home to beaver and otter so keep an eye on your dog and don't let them disturb these creatures or they will disappear. The day I was there we saw what we think was an otter. That's the nearest to the city I have ever seen one.

How To Get There

Get to the section of the Lougheed Highway (#7) that runs north-south between the Trans-Canada Highway (#1) (exit 44, just before the Port Mann Bridge) and where the Lougheed Highway and the Barnet Highway (#7A) meet.

The Western half is accessed by taking Colony Farm Road, which crosses the Lougheed just south of Pitt River Road, going east.

Both turnoffs from the highway have the distinctive GVRD green with yellow lettering signage, although it's hard to see the Western Half's sign until you're almost on top of it.

Hero's Rating: 🐾 🐾 🐾   **Human's Rating: ★ ★ ★**

Como Lake Park

Park Number	25
Trail Difficulty	1
Trail Condition	Excellent
Time	30 minutes

This park consists of a narrow strip of land surrounding a small lake. Just enough room for a path and a bit of lawn in a couple of places where it bulges out.

How To Get There
Take Como Lake Avenue. Turn south on Gatensbury Road.

Hero's Rating: 🐾   **Human's Rating:** ★

Coquitlam River Park

Park Number	26
Trail Difficulty	2
Trail Condition	Good to rustic
Time	2 hours

A strip of forest guards the river on both sides. Trails go along either bank, with one interruption on the east bank where you have to go around a bit of development and pick up the trail again. Locals told me that there is a waterfall that can be reached by going up the east side, higher than the Gabriola Street access I mention in the How To Get There section.

Parts of the trail are very well groomed crushed gravel and other parts are rustic and look like they will be swamped when the river is high, but you should still be able to get through.

On both sides of Patricia Street there is a pedestrian bridge across the river. You can walk down the west bank at least as far as the Lougheed. You can walk down the east bank all the way to **Colony Farm Regional Park**. It's all part of the **PoCo Trail**.

Water quality in the Coquitlam River is Fair.

How To Get There
There are many ways to get access to this park. Trails lead into it all along the river on both sides.

One way is to take the Lougheed Highway (#7) or the Barnet Highway (#7A) to where they meet by Coquitlam Centre. The street that continues north from this intersection is Pine Tree Way. Take this up to where it bears to the right on Pathan and then right again on Pipeline Road. Turn left on Gabriola and park at the end. Another way is to turn up Shaughnessy on the east side of the river, which takes you into the larger part of the park. There is an equestrian centre up here.

Hero's Rating: 🐾 🐾 🐾   **Human's Rating:** ★ ★ ★

Hoy Creek Linear Park

Park Number	27
Trail Difficulty	1
Trail Condition	Good
Time	30 minutes

Nice little ravine park complete with a rearing pond for salmon, which were in abundance on the November day we visited, as were the school kids watching the salmon spawn.

Water quality in Hoy Creek is Fair.

How To Get There

Take the Lougheed Highway or the Barnet Highway to where they meet by Coquitlam Centre. The street that continues on is Pine Tree Way. Take this north past **Town Centre Park** (Lafarge Lake) and turn left on Pinewood and left again on Delahaye. The Park starts here and goes south.

Hero's Rating: 🐾   **Human's Rating:** ★ ★

Kilmer Park

Park Number	28
Trail Difficulty	1
Trail Condition	Poor
Time	20 minutes

A small and unassuming little park with a few trails through a lightly wooded area behind an elementary school. There is a fairly long trail just behind (to the east of) this park that goes all the way down to the Mary Hill Bypass, but mind the industrial land to the east.

How To Get There

This trail can be accessed on Pooley and Connaught Drive. Access Pooley off Pitt River Road.

Hero's Rating: 🐾   **Human's Rating:** ★

Laurentian Park

Park Number	29
Trail Difficulty	2 - 3
Trail Condition	Good to Rustic
Time	5 - 30 minutes

Water

From behind the school on Montgomery, a wide trail runs across the creek to Laurentian Crescent. At the bottom of the ravine you can connect to deer trails which run up and down beside the creek.

How To Get There

Access Montgomery off Austin. Access Laurentian off Brunette or Austin.

Hero's Rating: 🐾 🐾   **Human's Rating:** ★

Minnekhada Regional Park

Park Number	30
Trail Difficulty	1 - 4
Trail Condition	Good to Rustic
Time	up to 6 hours

Drinking   Phone

Washroom   Water   Prohibited

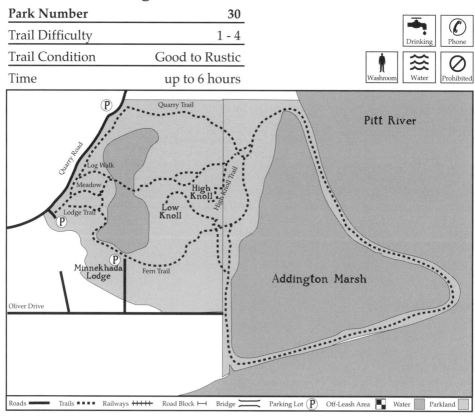

Roads ▬ Trails ■■■■ Railways ╫╫╫╫ Road Block ⊢⊣ Bridge ⤳ Parking Lot (P) Off-Leash Area 🏁 Water ▢ Parkland ▢

A truly excellent, forested park, one of the GVRD's finest, which says a lot, with a lovely little marsh hemmed in by hills that provide wonderful views out over the Pitt River. There are 8 km of trails in this park. Dogs are not allowed at the Lodge, which is closed in January.

The park borders the **Pitt-Addington Marsh Wildlife Management Area**, in fact, the two areas make one big park. You can easily stray from one park to the other, so be careful; the walk around the Addington Marsh is 3 hours in itself. The trails on the GVRD's side (Minnekhada) are extremely well marked with maps at every trail intersection.

How To Get There

From the Lougheed Highway, turn north on Coast Meridian Road. Two and a half km along this road, turn right onto Apel Drive. Follow the signs to the park entrance. Victoria Drive will take you to Quarry Road. Cedar Drive takes you to Oliver Road which goes to the Lodge parking lot.

Quarry Trail

Park Number	30
Trail Difficulty	1 - 2
Trail Condition	Good
Time	2 - 3 hours

From the Quarry Road parking lot keep bearing right and you will take Quarry Trail along by the road, circumnavigating the park in a clockwise direction. This trail climbs around the north end of the park and into the hills that separate this park from the **Pitt-Addington Marsh Wildlife Management Area**. This trail will allow you access to the **High Knoll Trail**, which is a bit of a climb but well worth it for the view. You can loop back through the **Mid Marsh Trail**, or follow the trail between **High Knoll** and **Low Knoll** to the **Fern Trail** and loop back past the lodge.

Hero's Rating: 🐾 🐾 🐾   **Human's Rating:** ★ ★ ★

High Knoll Trail

Park Number	30
Trail Difficulty	3 - 4
Trail Condition	Rustic
Time	30 minutes

Access this short climb off the north bit of the Quarry Trail. This is absolutely worth the climb; the view from the top is nothing less than spectacular, looking across Pitt River to Pitt Meadows.

Hero's Rating: 🐾 🐾   **Human's Rating:** ★ ★ ★ ★

Lodge Trail

Park Number	30
Trail Difficulty	1 - 2
Trail Condition	Good
Time	40 minutes

Connects Quarry Road parking lot to Minnekhada Lodge. Part of it runs along the Lower Marsh, close by the water.

Hero's Rating: 🐾 🐾 🐾   **Human's Rating:** ★ ★ ★

Fern Trail

Park Number	30
Trail Difficulty	1 - 3
Trail Condition	Good
Time	45 minutes

Starts at the picnic area and leads to the observation platform at Addington Lookout.

Hero's Rating: 🐾 🐾 🐾   **Human's Rating:** ★ ★

Mid Marsh Trail

Park Number	30
Trail Difficulty	1
Trail Condition	Good
Time	10 minutes

This trail crosses the marsh on a raised dyke, bringing you close to the water.

Hero's Rating: 🐾 🐾 🐾 🐾   **Human's Rating:** ★ ★ ★ ★

Meadow Trail and Log Walk

Park Number	30
Trail Difficulty	1
Trail Condition	Fair
Time	15 minutes

These trails connect the Quarry Trail with the Mid Marsh Trail. Both very muddy.

Hero's Rating: 🐾 🐾 🐾   **Human's Rating:** ★ ★

Mundy Park

Park Number	31
Trail Difficulty	1 - 2
Trail Condition	Excellent
Time	up to 1 hour

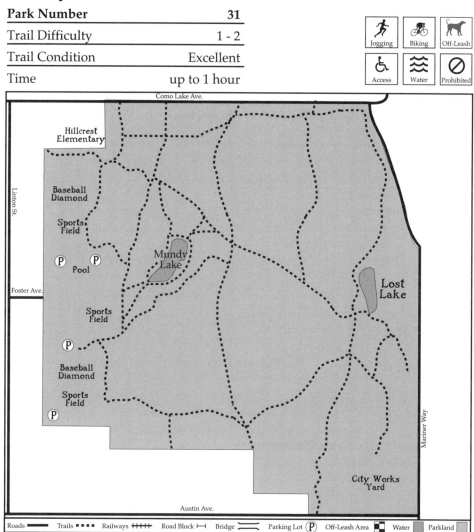

Very nice little park, mainly evergreen forest with some sizable trees. The trails are all similar; wide and well groomed. There are two lakes on the grounds; Mundy Lake, which has a path around it, and Lost Lake, which does not. Lots of water access, though the lakefronts can be very muddy. There is a map posted that lists many points of interest, even where all the stumps are in the park!

Late breaking news! There is an Off-Leash Area being planned for this park on a 6-month trial period. It is to be a fenced off meadow just north of Mundy Lake. The city is also considering allowing time-restricted Off-Leash access to the rest of the park as well.

How To Get There

Just to show how fast things change, when I surveyed this park I parked on the shoulder of Como Lake Avenue. Just before going to print I went back and there is a curb and "No Parking" signs all along there now. Linton Street (go south off Como Lake Avenue or north off Austin Avenue) will lead you to the main parking lots by the playing fields and disc golf course.

Hero's Rating: 🐾 🐾 🐾 🐾   **Human's Rating:** ★ ★ ★ ★

Pinecone Burke Provincial Park

Park Number	32
Trail Difficulty	1 - 5
Trail Condition	Good to poor
Time	Endless

A simply enormous park in the mountains north of Coquitlam, this area is less developed and less traveled than the North Shore Mountains, which it closely resembles. There are many trails going far into the wilderness that I look forward to exploring. But for a starter, here's one of the easier ones. See the appendix for the address of the Burke Mountain Naturalists for more information.

Woodland Walk Trail

Park Number	32
Trail Difficulty	1 - 3
Trail Condition	Good to poor
Time	2 - 3 hours

Near the end of Harper Road, a gravel road leads up the mountain. Follow this, taking the first left-hand fork. There are many, many small trails that head into the bush from this road, but there are also some good signs that will show you the way, so don't just go charging into the bush (like we did). You meet up with the powerlines, follow beside them, then meet them again, before turning up from what is still a road onto a footpath leading through the trees. Watch for the brightly coloured tape to keep on track. The trail does a loop with a side excursion up to a creek where there is an "Old Bridge." If what we got to was this artifact, then it's more "old" than "bridge" and I would strongly advise against crossing it. Just upstream from the bridge are several lovely waterfalls and pools.

How To Get There
Take the Lougheed Highway (#7) to Port Coquitlam and get onto Coast Meridian Road. At the top of Coast Meridian, take a right onto Harper, which is a gravel road. Follow Harper for 2 km to the gated access road on your right, just before the gun club.

Hero's Rating: 🐾 🐾 🐾   **Human's Rating:** ★ ★ ★ ★

Pitt-Addington Marsh Wildlife Management Area

(See **Addington Marsh** for Coquitlam side and **Grant Narrows Regional Park** for Pitt Meadows side)

PoCo Trail

Park Number	33
Trail Difficulty	1 - 3
Trail Condition	Excellent to poor
Time	Endless

Fishing | Swimming | Biking | Drinking | Phone

Horses | Jogging | Access | Washroom | Water | Prohibited

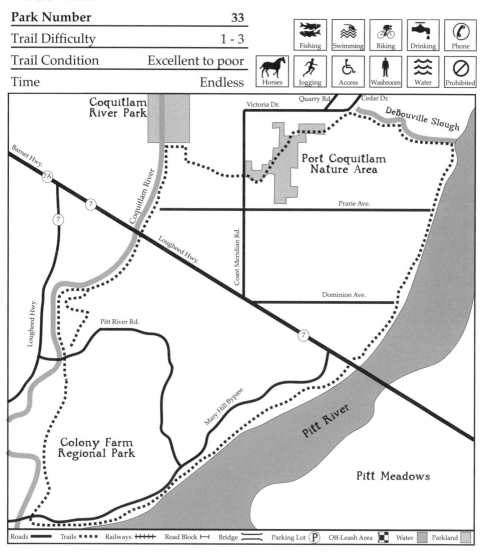

Roads ▬▬ Trails ▪▪▪▪ Railways ╬╬╬╬ Road Block ⊢⊣ Bridge ⟩⟨ Parking Lot Ⓟ Off-Leash Area ▣ Water ▨ Parkland ▨

This trail traces an enormous circle around Port Coquitlam, some of it in parks, some on roads. I do not have the space to tell you about every nuance, but here are the highlights. The map should be able to guide you in between the areas I talk about. See also **Colony Farm Regional Park**, and **Coquitlam River Park**, both of which form a part of the PoCo Trail.

How To Get There
See map for the many access points.

Coquitlam River Section

Park Number	33
Trail Difficulty	1 - 2
Trail Condition	Good to rustic
Time	1 - 4 hours

The trail starts around Patricia on the east side of Coquitlam River. A nice broad trail follows the river down past the Lougheed Highway and then crosses Pitt River Road before passing through First Nations land to **Colony Farm Regional Park**. Pedestrians are requested to stay on the dyke, as the reserve is private land. Hero loves this river because he likes to wade, not swim, and the Coquitlam has a shallow gravelly bed. The long roads on the lower half would be good to cycle.

Water quality in the Coquitlam River is Fair.

Hero's Rating: 🐾 🐾 🐾   **Human's Rating:** ★ ★

Pitt River Dyke

Park Number	33
Trail Difficulty	1
Trail Condition	Excellent
Time	1 - 4 hours

This is a typical flat, wide dyke trail, great for biking or walking. The bit south of the Lougheed is quite industrial, but the part north of the Lougheed is mostly farmland and quite pretty. The northern terminus of this walk turns west on the DeBouville Slough, then east again to **Minnekhada Regional Park** and the **(Pitt) Addington Marsh**.

Water quality in the Pitt River is Good.

Hero's Rating: 🐾 🐾 🐾   **Human's Rating:** ★ ★ ★

Port Coquitlam Nature Area

Park Number	33
Trail Difficulty	1
Trail Condition	Excellent
Time	30 minutes

With a name like that you expect something wilder than this park. It's just a bit of bush with a medium-sized creek running through it. Quite nice, but very tame. The main trail starts at the Hyde Creek Recreation Centre and follows the creek north to Cedar.

Hero's Rating: 🐾 🐾   **Human's Rating:** ★

Riverview

Park Number	34
Trail Difficulty	1 - 2
Trail Condition	Good
Time	30 minutes

There is a gravel road that runs across the back of the Riverview grounds. There are also several fairly large fields dotted with trees, the largest of these toward the south of the grounds. There is a quaint, old orchard and a terraced, formal garden, with a small pond, called Fennie's Garden.

You can see across **Colony Farm Regional Park**.

How To Get There

I have heard tell of places to park around back (to the west) of Riverview, but they weren't evident. Take Lougheed Highway (#7) southwest from its interchange with the Barnet Highway (#7A). Take the first entrance to Riverview and park in the top parking area.

Hero's Rating: 🐾 🐾   **Human's Rating:** ★ ★

Town Centre Park (Lafarge Lake)

Park Number	35
Trail Difficulty	1
Trail Condition	Excellent
Time	15 minutes

A trail circles the lake and adjacent lawns. Looks like a pretty new park. Give it some time and it may turn out better.

How To Get There

Get to the section of the Lougheed Highway (#7) that runs north-south between the Trans-Canada Highway (#1) (exit 44, just before the Port Mann Bridge) and where the Lougheed Highway and the Barnet Highway (#7A) meet. The street that continues on is Pine Tree Way. The park is in the school and recreation complex.

Hero's Rating: No Paws   **Human's Rating: No Stars**

Delta

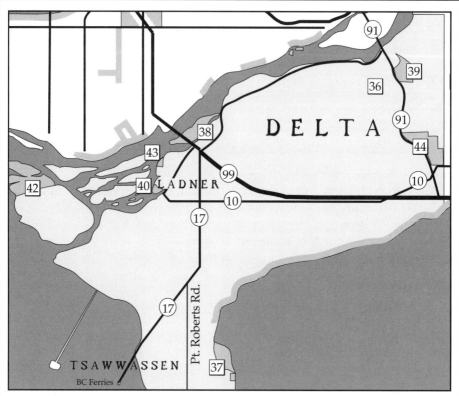

The Boundary Bay dykes go on for miles.

Delta

True to its name, Delta sports a unique low-lying topography in the GVRD, including Burns Bog and some interesting Fraser River environments, as well as miles of dykes on Mud Bay.

Burns Bog

Park Number	36
Trail Difficulty	1
Trail Condition	Excellent to good
Time	2 hour tours

Burns Bog is an environmental refuge and you can only go in there on guided tours, which run July through September. You are allowed to take your dog on these tours, on-leash of course. When the weather is wet the trail can be very wet as well.

To find out about touring Burns Bog call the Burns Bog Conservation Society, at 572-0373.

Myself, I prefer self-guided outings, so I'd rather go to the **Delta Nature Reserve**, which is a small part of Burns Bog that has been cut off from the rest of the bog by the highway.

How To Get There
Please call first to book a tour.

Hero's Rating: 🐾   **Human's Rating:** ★ ★ ★

Boundary Bay Regional Park

Park Number	37
Trail Difficulty	1
Trail Condition	Good to fair
Time	1 - 2 hours

Boundary Bay Regional Park is situated on the east side of the peninsula, and houses the Tsawassen Ferry Terminal on its west side. The park also includes a dyke that lines Boundary Bay.

Here's a great place to walk your dog on the beach. According to one local, there are times in the winter when the GVRD wants you to stay off the beach due to shorebirds, but in the summer, when most other beaches are closed to dogs, this one is open. The bathing area (Centennial Beach, which is off-limits to dogs) is south of the part of the park that contains the trails.

Above the beach there is a grassy/marshy area with a few trails crisscrossing it. Some of the little marshy pools contain water which will make your dog smell simply dreadful, but I think this is a natural occurrence, rather than pollution, and you can send your dog into the ocean to clean off before you go back to the car.

Water quality in Boundary Bay is Fair.

How To Get There

From Highway #99 take the Tsawassen Ferry Road (Highway #17). Before you get to the ferry terminal, turn left on 56th Street, also known as Point Roberts Road. A left on 12th Avenue will get you to the north end of the park, or continue with a right along Boundary Bay Road and go to the main entrance by the bathing beach.

Hero's Rating: 🐾 🐾 🐾 🐾   **Human's Rating:** ★ ★ ★

Boundary Bay Dykes

Park Number	37
Trail Difficulty	1
Trail Condition	Excellent to good
Time	up to 4 hours

There is a dyke system that circles northeast from near Boundary Bay Regional Park, and goes east almost around Mud Bay. This is a great place to walk for those who really want to get out and stretch those muscles. Even for bike riders this dyke just goes on forever. At the Delta-Surrey border, the dyke runs very close to the highway for some distance. Nearing the **Serpentine Fen** area, the dyke runs into a railway. While it is possible to cross this, the public/private status of the dyke on the other side is questionable, and once you get to the Serpentine, the mud is unbelievable. Best to turn around, either at the narrowing mentioned above or at the railroad.

There are irrigation canals (that you may want to keep your dog out of) between the dyke and farmer's fields (which you should definitely keep your dog out of). In these ditches is some of the foulest, nastiest smelling, brown muddy gunk that Hero has dragged home so far.

Water quality in Boundary Bay is Fair.

How To Get There

Directions to **Boundary Bay Regional Park** will get you to Boundary Bay where the south end of the walk starts at 17A Avenue and Beachgrove Road. You can also access the dyke at quite a few points by traveling south on any of several roads which intersect the Ladner Trunk Road (Highway #10); 64th Street, 72nd Street, 88th Street, etc.

Hero's Rating: 🐾 🐾 🐾   **Human's Rating:** ★ ★ ★ ★

Deas Island Regional Park

Park Number	38
Trail Difficulty	1
Trail Condition	Good
Time	2 hours

Horses | Fishing | Drinking | Phone

Jogging | Access | Washroom | Water | Prohibited

Roads ▬▬ Trails ▪▪▪▪ Railways ┼┼┼┼ Road Block ┣━┫ Bridge ══ Parking Lot Ⓟ Off-Leash Area ◼ Water ▣ Parkland ▢

There are over 5 km of shoreline trails on Deas Island through a light forest. The Fraser River is on one side, with industrial development, but the view is a little nicer on the Deas Slough side, to the east. The island is covered with deciduous trees, tall grasses, and a forest of horsetail. There are a couple of grassy fields, although one of them is a picnic area. There is a group camping area that can be booked through the GVRD. There is no biking allowed.

Leaving from the first parking lot, **Tinmaker's Walk** will take you along the west side of the island on a wide, flat path. Bear right and you will follow **Riverside Walk** to the **Island Tip Trail**, which will take you to the southwest end of the island. On your way back you can bear right again to the **Sand Dune Trail,** and right again to get onto the part of the **Dyke Loop Trail** that goes to the east side of the island and the **Slough View Trail.** Be careful making your connection from the **Sand Dune Trail** to the **Dyke Loop Trail**; there is a bunch of deer trails through the horsetails that lead into the bush and not much of anywhere else.

Hero liked the open meadows and the river access. The view across the slough would be nice even if it didn't rhyme.

Water quality in the Fraser River Main Arm is Fair.

How To Get There

From Highway #99, take the River Road exit (#28) at the south end of the George Massey Tunnel and travel east 2.5 km.

From Highway #91, take the River Road exit just south of the Alex Fraser Bridge and go west on River Road. In about 8 km you will pass Chapman Industries. Follow park signs.

There are two parking lots, the one you come to immediately and one half way up the island at Fisher's Field Picnic Area.

Hero's Rating: 🐾 🐾   **Human's Rating: ★ ★**

Delta Nature Reserve

Park Number	39
Trail Difficulty	1
Trail Condition	Excellent to good
Time	2 - 3 hours

This park is physically a part of **Burns Bog**, or would be if the highway didn't cut between them, but it is not so restricted as the Bog proper. The flora of the bog is quite different from a lot of other ecosystems in the GVRD, and well worth a look.

There is a gravel road that basically follows the railway, right through the park and down past 64th Avenue to where **Watershed Park** begins. A fairly deep and swift running creek with a sandy bed follows the same route.

A number of looped excursion trails feed off the main trail and enter the bog. They are boardwalked in the more soggy sections. I was there last in January and the ground was still quite navigable. Lots of mud for your dog, however.

How To Get There

Heading south over the Alex Fraser Bridge, take the first exit off the bridge that curves to the right. You will end up going north on Nordell Way. Don't go into the commercial vehicles scales, go straight toward River Road another block, turning right at Nordell Court. This will take you back under the highway to the Great Pacific Forum. There is a trail that starts as a brick path at the northeast corner of the parking lot, and heads under an overpass to the right.

Hero's Rating: 🐾 🐾 🐾   **Human's Rating: ★ ★ ★**

Ladner Harbour Park

Park Number	40
Trail Difficulty	1
Trail Condition	Fair to Poor
Time	30 minutes

The park has a playground and picnic area around a lawn. There are trails to the east of this, which tend to be flooded at high tide, and a viewing platform at the far end. There's a lot of garbage around. This park is immediately adjacent to the **South Arm Marshes Wildlife Management Area**.

Water quality in the Fraser River Main Arm is Fair.

How To Get There

Traveling south on Highway #99, go through the Deas Island Tunnel and take your first right onto River Road west. This part of River Road does not connect with the bit that runs across the north edge of Delta. You can also approach this by taking Highway #10 through Ladner, turn right on Elliot and right on River.

Look for a street sign that says Ladner Harbour park. Follow this road (east) to the parking lot.

Hero's Rating: 🐾 🐾   **Human's Rating:** ★

Purfleet Point Reserve (Annacis Island)

Park Number	41
Trail Difficulty	1
Trail Condition	Fair
Time	10 minutes

A horseshoe shaped walk around a marshy canal, surrounded by the Fraser River. Lots of water access. A bit mucky. Lots of garbage.

Water quality in the Fraser River Main Arm is Fair.

How To Get There

From New Westminster take the Queensbourough Bridge to Annacis Island. Follow Derwent or Cliveden east to where they end. The walk is around the eastern tip of the island.

Hero's Rating: 🐾 🐾   **Human's Rating:** ★

Reifel Migratory Bird Sanctuary

Park Number	42
Trail Difficulty	1
Trail Condition	Good
Time	1 - 2 hours

Understandably, due to environmental sensitivity of the park, dogs are not allowed.

South Arm Marshes Wildlife Management Area

Park Number	43
Trail Difficulty	1
Trail Condition	Good to fair
Time	1 hour

The park actually covers a number of islands in the South Arm of the Fraser, but we'll just deal with some trails you can reach by car. There are a couple of trails by **Ladner Harbour Park**, that are at least a bit nicer than the ones at that park, but the nicest are a short drive south of that, by the Ladner Public Boat Launch. There are two access points through the chain-link fence, and when the tide is high, the bridges between the two areas can be under water.

Except for a slight methane smell this is a very pleasant park. The trails wander along canals and pools through a deciduous forest, the branches often filled with bald eagles. There is a tall viewing platform looking over a large inaccessible section of the marsh. Herons, ducks, and merganzers are among the birds you are likely to see here. Please watch that your dog does not disturb the wildlife, especially around nesting season.

Water quality in the Fraser River Main Arm is Fair.

How To Get There

Traveling south on Highway #99, go through the Deas Island Tunnel and take your first right onto River Road west. This part of River Road does not connect with the bit that runs across the top of Delta. You can also approach this by taking Highway #10 through Ladner, turn right on Elliot and right on River.

Look for a road called Ferry that branches off to the northeast and follow this almost to the end.

Hero's Rating: 🐾 🐾 🐾   **Human's Rating:** ★ ★ ★

Watershed Park Reserve

Park Number	**44**
Trail Difficulty	1 - 3
Trail Condition	Good to poor
Time	1 - 3 hours

The trails in this park range from a couple of wide roads to trails that have been created mainly by mountain bikers. There are many small trails that wind and circle in a veritable maze, so be careful. One of the larger roads runs from 64th and Highway #91 through the park to where Ladner Trunk Road becomes 58th.

This park has a complex forest of fairly old evergreens, as well as mossy stands of maple and birch or alder. There are many little streams and pools of collected rainwater. It is unexpectedly hilly for a park in Delta, but this is where the land climbs out of the flatlands.

There are a couple of fire pits in this park, one of which has a covered picnic area with what looks like a covered cooking facility being built.

How To Get There

From Highway #91, north of Highway #99 and south of the Alex Fraser Bridge, turn east on 64th Avenue (also called Kitson Parkway). After a complex of condos, watch on your right for trailheads.

You can walk to this park from the **Delta Nature Reserve**. Just follow the main trail under the 64th Avenue interchange, (watch for broken glass here) then take the path that leads up to the road. Follow 64th east.

Hero's Rating: 🐾 🐾 🐾   **Human's Rating:** ★ ★

Langley

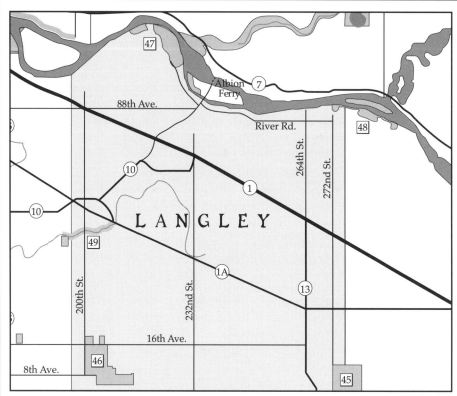

Mt. Baker from Campbell Valley Regional Park's Off-Leash Area.

Langley

Langley sports no fewer than four regional parks, two of which hug the Fraser River with good dyke walks. Parts of Langley are still partly undeveloped, or remain in the agricultural land reserve, giving walkers a glimpse of farm life.

Aldergrove Lake Regional Park

Park Number	45
Trail Difficulty	1 - 2
Trail Condition	Good to fair
Time	5 hours

Swimming	Biking	Drinking	Phone	Off-Leash
Horses	Jogging	Access	Washroom	Water	Prohibited

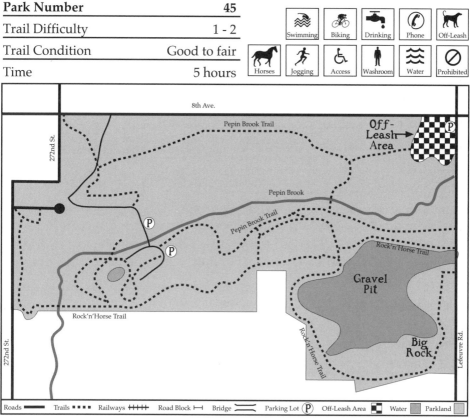

| Roads ━━ | Trails ▪▪▪▪ | Railways ┼┼┼┼ | Road Block ⊢⊣ | Bridge ⩵ | Parking Lot Ⓟ | Off-Leash Area ▨ | Water ▨ | Parkland ▨ |

Nice enough park, but unfortunately the GVRD found out after purchasing the park that someone else owned gravel rights to the land. There is, therefore, a large gravel pit, which the Rock'n'Horse Trail circumnavigates, and the small lake near the picnic area is a featureless almost perfectly round man-made thing of sand.

How To Get There

From Trans-Canada Highway (#1) or Fraser Highway (#1A) take the 264th Street exit (exit #73 on the Trans-Canada) which is the Aldergrove–Bellingham

Highway (#13) and go south. Turn left on Warner Road (8th Avenue). Watch for the Main entrance, or proceed past the main entrance and turn right on Lefeuvre Road, to the Off-Leash Area.

Off-Leash Area

Park Number	45
Trail Difficulty	1
Trail Condition	Good
Time	10 minutes

There is an Off-Leash Area at the northeast corner of the park, off Lefeuvre Road. This consists of an open field and a bit of trail taking you to the Pepin Brook Trail.

Hero's Rating: 🐾 🐾 🐾 🐾   **Human's Rating:** ★ ★

The Pepin Brook Trail

Park Number	45
Trail Difficulty	1 - 2
Trail Condition	Good
Time	1 hour

Pepin Brook is home to the Salish Sucker, an endangered fish. Please keep your dog out of this creek and the marshes that surround it.

The **Pepin Brook Trail** (4 km) follows the brook from the Off-Leash Area, around to the lake and back to Lefeuvre Road. Dogs are not permitted on the beach area.

Hero's Rating: 🐾 🐾   **Human's Rating:** ★ ★

The Rock 'n' Horse Trail

Park Number	45
Trail Difficulty	1 - 2
Trail Condition	Fair
Time	2 hours

The **Rock 'n' Horse Trail** (7 km) is used by cyclists, hikers, and horses; pedestrians yield to equestrians, cyclists yield to pedestrians and equestrians. There is a large rock on the course which was deposited by glaciers 12,000 years ago. The trail circles a large gravel extraction pit.

Hero's Rating: 🐾 🐾   **Human's Rating:** ★ ★

Campbell Valley Regional Park

Park Number	**46**
Trail Difficulty	1
Trail Condition	Excellent to fair
Time	5 hours

Drinking | Phone | Off-Leash

Horses | Washroom | Water | Prohibited

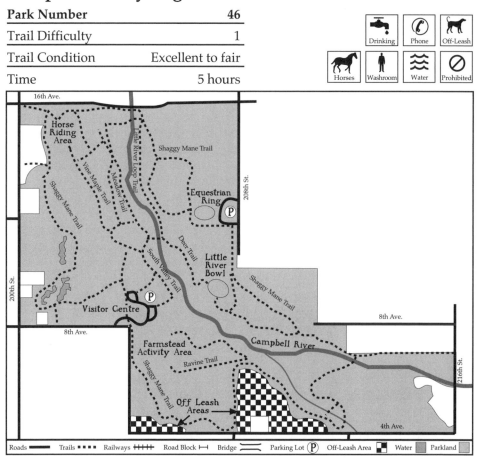

Roads ▬▬   Trails ▪▪▪▪   Railways ┼┼┼┼   Road Block ⊢⊣   Bridge ═══   Parking Lot Ⓟ   Off-Leash Area ▦   Water ▮   Parkland ▮

There are a number of rustic trails that dog walkers may prefer to the more traveled routes. Be aware that there are equestrian areas in this park including a cross-country route with jumps. There will obviously be horses traveling at speed here and a poorly placed barking dog might cause an upset.

Water quality in the Little Campbell River is Fair.

How To Get There

From Trans-Canada Highway (#1) take the Langley City–200th Street South exit (#58). Travel south and turn east on 16th Avenue. Look for the signs to the North Valley entrance and the Campbell Valley Equestrian Centre.

Or, to reach the Off-Leash Area, continue on 200th to 8th Avenue for the South Valley entrance and the Old Orchard picnic area and Visitor Centre. You can walk the Shaggy Mane trail (with leash on) from here to the Off-Leash Area.

From Highway #99 take the 8th Avenue exit (#2) and proceed east on 8th to 200th, then as above.

Off-Leash Areas

Park Number	46
Trail Difficulty	1
Trail Condition	Good
Time	1 hour

There are two Off-Leash Areas being tested in this park, both are off 4th Avenue, along the Shaggy Mane trail, but the larger one is only in effect September through April. Neither are very well marked, so refer to the map. Both are basically open fields, which is great if you have a dog that will fetch or a couple of dogs that will chase each other, and lousy if you want to go for a nice walk along trails with your dog. For myself, walking aimlessly through open fields just doesn't do it for me the way traversing a trail does. In almost any weather your feet will quickly become soaked from the tall grasses. The larger of the two Off-Leash Areas has a great view of Mount Baker. There is no water to be had at either of these areas but there is a creek nearby, with a "water splash" for the horses, which Hero found deep enough to lie down in.

Hero's Rating: 🐾 🐾 🐾   **Human's Rating:** ★ ★ ★

Shaggy Mane Trail

Park Number	46
Trail Difficulty	1
Trail Condition	Good
Time	1 - 3 hours

Be extremely courteous to equestrians. If your dog is one to go after horses, best to not use this trail. Unfortunately this trail is practically unavoidable as it is your access to the Off-Leash Areas. Well used by horses and liberally littered with their scat.

Hero's Rating: 🐾 🐾   **Human's Rating:** ★ ★

Deer Trail

Park Number	46
Trail Difficulty	1
Trail Condition	Fair
Time	30 minutes

The Deer Trail (not just a deer trail, which in the lexicon of this book is an uncultured trail worn by the feet of animals or people) is a quiet little rustic trail which runs through the old Little River Bowl. A nice alternative to the Shaggy Mane trail, though muddier, it takes you away from the equestrian ring.

Hero's Rating: 🐾 🐾   **Human's Rating:** ★ ★ ★

Ravine Trail

Park Number	46
Trail Difficulty	1
Trail Condition	Good
Time	40 minutes

The ravine trail loops quickly from the farmstead to the creek and back again.

Hero's Rating: 🐾 🐾   **Human's Rating:** ★ ★

Little River Loop Trail and South Valley Trail

Park Number	46
Trail Difficulty	1
Trail Condition	Excellent
Time	45 minutes

This trail is very well groomed and level, with boardwalks over some sections. You can make a circle from the 16th Street parking lot or you can take the South Valley trail from the 8th Avenue lot.

Hero's Rating: 🐾 🐾 🐾   **Human's Rating:** ★ ★ ★

Vine Maple Trail and Meadow Trail

Park Number	46
Trail Difficulty	1
Trail Condition	Fair
Time	30 minutes

Either way you go you can also take in a couple of the side trails; Vine Maple or Meadow Trails, which are a little more rustic and wind through vine and broad-leaf maples, with one great granddaddy of a broadleaf maple at the south end, just before they run into the South Valley Trail.

Hero's Rating: 🐾 🐾 🐾   **Human's Rating:** ★ ★ ★

Derby Reach Regional Park

Park Number	47
Trail Difficulty	1 - 3
Trail Condition	Excellent to good
Time	6 hours

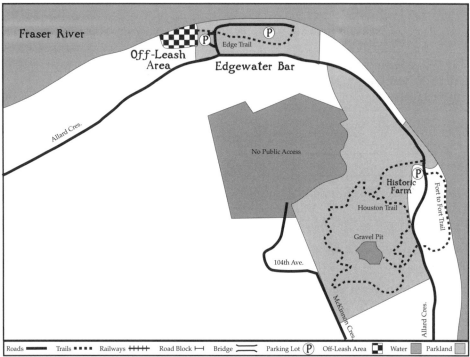

Derby Reach is on the Fraser River. The two Derby Reach sites are quite dissimilar, so they are described separately.

Water quality in the Fraser River here is Good.

How To Get There

From Trans-Canada Highway (#1) take the 200th St. exit (#58) north. Take a right on 88th Avenue. Turn Left on 108th Street. Go right on Allard Crescent, which goes through the park. The Historic Farm Site is encountered first, or if you continue you reach Edgewater Bar.

From Fort Langley you can take Wilson Crescent which becomes McKinnon Crescent. Turn right on Allard Crescent.

Historic Farm Site

The site has a collection of old farm buildings.

Houston Trail

Park Number	47
Trail Difficulty	1 - 3
Trail Condition	Good
Time	1 hour

Can be accessed from the Historic Farm lot on Allard Crescent or from the parking lot on McKinnon. Please note that this trail is shared with equestrians. Mixed forest of evergreens and mossy deciduous. You should keep your dog from the nearby marshes, for the sake of the animal life there, as well as for the fact that they are quite muddy.

Hero's Rating: 🐾 🐾 🐾   **Human's Rating:** ★ ★ ★

Fort to Fort Trail

Park Number	47
Trail Difficulty	1
Trail Condition	Excellent
Time	30 minutes

Starts on the river side of the road at the Historic Farm parking lot on Allard Crescent and goes south along the high bank, past some lovely pastures and a duck pond. Nice views of far shore (you can see **Kanaka Creek**) and mountains behind, with Baker in the distance to the south.

Hero's Rating: 🐾 🐾   **Human's Rating:** ★ ★ ★

Edgewater Bar

This park has great places for people to camp right at the side of the river, and fish.

Water quality in the Fraser River here is Good.

Off-Leash Area

Park Number	47
Trail Difficulty	1
Trail Condition	Good
Time	15 minutes

To the west of the entrance there is a pretty nice Off-Leash Area. There's a small grassy field to run on and a beach for water access.

Hero's Rating: 🐾 🐾 🐾   **Human's Rating:** ★ ★

Edge Trail

Park Number	47
Trail Difficulty	1
Trail Condition	Good
Time	15 minutes

A very short jaunt through the woods behind the camping spots. Watch for anglers at the water's edge.

Hero's Rating: 🐾   **Human's Rating:** ★

Glen Valley Regional Park
Poplar Bar

Park Number	48
Trail Difficulty	1
Trail Condition	Fair
Time	30 minutes

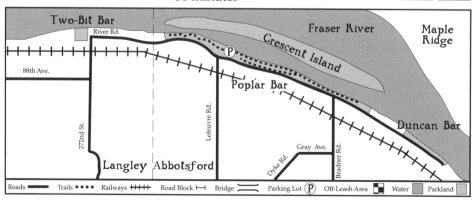

A short walk by the river. Nice views of Crescent Island and the far shore and mountains in the distance. This park is mainly for fishing, and it is mostly in Matsqui, but it is best reached through Langley, which is why it's in this section. Water quality in the Fraser River here is Good.

How To Get There

From Trans-Canada Highway (#1) take the 264th Street exit (#73) north. Follow 264th (also known as County Line) to River Road. Turn right (east) on River and the left (south) on 272nd Street.

From Fort Langley you can also access River Road, sometimes called 88th.

At Two-Bit Bar, there is a parking lot, but the park itself is very small. Turn right along River Road and proceed to Poplar Bar. Here there is another parking lot and a few trails. If you continue on River Road you can park on the side of the road by Duncan Bar, but make sure to leave enough room for farm vehicles to get through, and park well away from gates (imagine a large tractor towing a trailer turning through this gate onto the road).

Hero's Rating: 🐾 🐾   **Human's Rating:** ★ ★

Nicomekl River Park

Park Number		49
Trail Difficulty		1
Trail Condition		Good
Time		1 - 2 hours

This park is actually made up of several parks; the Nicomekl Flood Plain Park, Portage Park, and Brydon Park Nature Reserve, and stretches from where 208th Street meets the Fraser Highway and the Langley Bypass to meet up with **High Knoll Park** on the Surrey/Langley Border. The Nicomekl River runs through it, and paths run alongside the river through tall grasses, mainly on the south side of the river. The area teems with waterfowl.

Brydon Park Nature Reserve is a smallish lake right on the border with Surrey. There are trails around this, and you may enter with your dog, but strictly on-leash. Just south of this park a wide trail runs between it and Nicomekl Park.

Water quality in the Nicomekl River is Fair.

How To Get There

Though you can access the park at various places along its length, the only official parking lot is at a small picnic area at the eastern end, off 208th. 200th Street will get you there, and turning off at 53rd or thereabouts will get you in the general vicinity, and then you can park on the street.

Hero's Rating: 🐾 🐾 🐾   **Human's Rating:** ★ ★

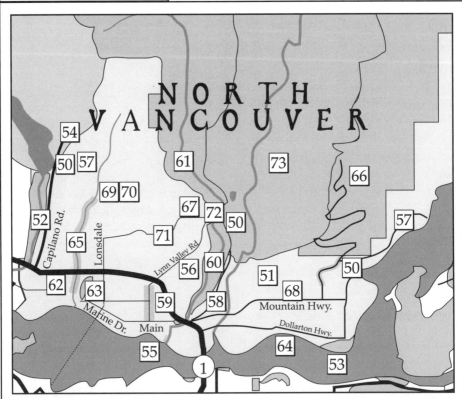

NORTH VANCOUVER

54

50 57

69 70

61

73

66

52

Capilano Rd.

65

Lonsdale

67 72

50

71

57

62

63

56 60

51

50

59

58

68

Mountain Hwy.

Marine Dr.

Main

Dollarton Hwy.

55

1

64

53

Lynn Valley Rd

Mucking about down the Seymour River.

North Vancouver

Having been born and raised in North Vancouver, I am naturally biased, but the canyons and mountainous forests of the North Shore have their own special magic and are the very best places in the entire world to walk your dog. North Vancouver District is one of the leading municipalities in designating really great Off-Leash Areas.

North Shore Mountain Trails

There are several trails on the North Shore that run across the south side of the mountains, through dense evergreen forest, and above the line where houses have been built (thus far) in North and West Vancouver. Many of them cross through other parks such as **Lynn Canyon**, **Mount Seymour Provincial Park**, and **Capilano River Regional Park**, and they all intertwine as they cross the mountains.

The **Bridle Trail, Pipeline Road,** and **Powerlines Trail** all crisscross and intersect with the **Baden-Powell** (For the eastern part of the Baden-Powell see under this heading in West Vancouver).

It is very easy to mix and match these trails, going up one trail, coming back down the other and still arriving at your car. It is also, apparently, quite easy to get lost.

In addition there are smaller deer trails that are increasingly being used by cyclists which in turn makes them more substantial trails. These trails are generally quite rustic, overgrown, and poorly marked in some instances. They can lead you astray if you are not careful. Eventually, they will take you back to one of the larger trails, but it might take some doing to get back to where you parked your car.

All of these trails run through dense evergreen forests, some of which is first growth.

Baden-Powell Trail

Park Number	**50**
Trail Difficulty	1 - 5
Trail Condition	Excellent to rustic
Time	Endless

Biking	Drinking	Phone	Off-Leash
Fishing	Washroom	Water	Prohibited

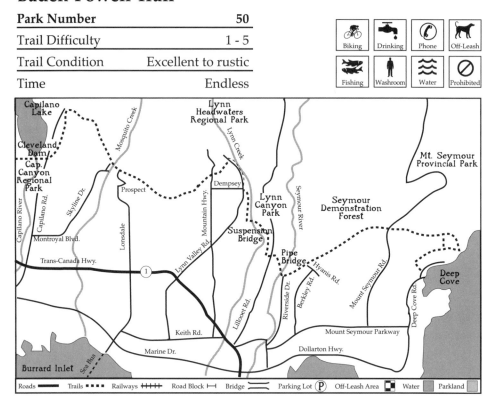

Roads ▬▬ Trails ▪▪▪▪ Railways ┼┼┼┼ Road Block ⊢⊣ Bridge ═══ Parking Lot Ⓟ Off-Leash Area ▣ Water ▮ Parkland ▒

The Baden-Powell Trail is the longest and best known of the North Shore Trails, and it is Off-Leash the whole way (except, technically, where it crosses **Mount Seymour Provincial Park**). It runs all the way from Deep Cove at the east end of North Van to Horseshoe Bay at the west end of West Van. Baden-Powell was, of course, the guy who founded the Boy Scouts (and no immediate relation to the author).

There are many trail accesses to the Baden-Powell. It was built to be done as many day hikes as opposed to all at one go. The trail has bright orange flashings marking the way, some with a fleur-de-lis and "BP" marked on them in blue. There has been some very recent signage added to parts of the trail; nice signposts with maps and "you are here" markers at trail intersections.

I am going to assume that your party has only one car and so all hikes are going to be ones you can do there and back again. It's pretty easy to string a couple hikes together if you want to plant a car at either end.

Deep Cove to Seymour Mushroom

Park Number	50
Trail Difficulty	4 - 5
Trail Condition	Good to rustic
Time	3 - 4 hours

 Biking

 Off-Leash

Fishing

Water

Starting in Deep Cove, (pretty well all the amenities are here) the trail climbs steeply, leading northeast up Indian Arm before heading on its eventual westerly way. There is a shortcut which circumvents most of this little horseshoe—watch carefully for yellow flashings, or you'll miss it. But you will also miss a very nice, rock bluff lookout over Indian Arm and Belcarra.

When leaving the lookout be careful you don't lose the trail as it crosses the powerlines. If you do, however, you can walk up the powerlines to Indian River Road, which is where the trail goes too. Lots of berries on the powerlines in the spring, and lots of bears! Here I discovered to my relief that Hero would indeed come back when called away from chasing a bear. Good boy! (Yes, Bessie, you came back too, good girl!)

Follow Indian River Road west until you hook up with the next trailhead. This climbs and cuts across Mount Seymour Road (the road that climbs Mount Seymour to the ski runs). Technically, where it crosses **Mount Seymour Provincial Park** the trail is no longer Off-Leash. Proceed onward and you will come to a spot where the BP takes a plunge through the forest from the fairly substantial dirt road which you have been on.

A small detour will take you to the Seymour "Mushroom." In the old days they would choose a likely tall stump and top it with a circular roof to provide folks with a little shelter on the trail. There were several of these on the North Shore at one time. This one has all but rotted away and is enshrined by a little picket fence and an informational sign telling you about the artifact. North Van's answer to ruins.

How To Get There

Heading west on the Trans-Canada Highway (#1) take the very first exit (#23B) off the Second Narrows Bridge. This is Main Street which turns into the old Dollarton Highway, the scenic route to Deep Cove.

Or, from the Trans-Canada Highway (#1) take exit #22. If you have been traveling eastbound take the overpass on the left across the highway.

Near the Superstore, turn right onto Mount Seymour Parkway, then take Mount Seymour Parkway to Dollarton, then turn left. This will take you to Deep Cove, where, by the way, there are several excellent restaurants.

The trailhead is just past Panorama Park on Panorama Drive. Take a left off Deep Cove Road once you reach the village.

Hero's Rating: 🐾 🐾 🐾   **Human's Rating:** ★ ★ ★ ★

Suspension Bridge to Seymour Mushroom

Park Number	50
Trail Difficulty	4 - 5
Trail Condition	Excellent to rustic
Time	3 - 4 hours

The beginning of this hike is the Lynn Canyon Suspension Bridge, hung on cables over a deep chasm. This alone is worth the trip, but you have a good hike ahead of you as well, heading south and then east. Note that the area immediately surrounding the suspension bridge down to Twin Falls is not off-leash. Take care around the canyon edges, people fall here every year.

The trail bears to the right and downstream, dipping to the creek a couple of times, then climbs up from the water and heads east, crossing Lillooet Road before some stairs descend to cross the Seymour River on a pipe bridge. A small section continues through a corridor lined with houses, up to Hyannis. From here it climbs steeply through excellent forests to the Seymour Mushroom.

Water quality in Lynn Creek is Good.

WARNING: The river current can be very strong. See **About Rivers** in the Trail Wisdom section of the book.

How To Get There

From the Trans-Canada Highway (#1) in either direction take exit #19 (Lynn Valley Road) and follow Lynn Valley Road northeast. Watch for a sign to **Lynn Canyon Park** on the right side of the road. Follow the signs (on Peters Road) to the parking lot.

Hero's Rating: 🐾 🐾 🐾 🐾   **Human's Rating:** ★ ★ ★ ★

Suspension Bridge to Lynn Valley Road

Park Number	50
Trail Difficulty	3 - 4
Trail Condition	Rustic
Time	1 hour

A short section that can be easily walked in an hour or so. The path leaves right from the upstream side of the suspension bridge's west end. Note that the area immediately surrounding the suspension bridge is not off-leash. The trail plunges into the chasm and then meanders along by the creek on occasional boardwalks. When the water is low, there are rocky beaches accessible from this path. Finally the path climbs to Lynn Valley Road. Don't let your dog run ahead of you because the path empties directly onto the road, which can be quite busy.

Water quality in Lynn Creek is Good.

WARNING: The river current can be very strong. See **About Rivers** in the Trail Wisdom section of the book.

How To Get There

From the Trans-Canada Highway (#1) in either direction take exit #19 (Lynn Valley Road) and follow Lynn Valley Road northeast. Watch for a sign to **Lynn Canyon Park** on the right side of the road. Follow the signs (Peters Road) to the parking lot.

Hero's Rating: 🐾 🐾 🐾   **Human's Rating:** ★ ★ ★

Rice Lake Road Trail

For a connecting trail that is not officially part of the Baden-Powell, see under this heading.

Lynn Valley Road to Skyline Drive

Park Number	50
Trail Difficulty	3 - 4
Trail Condition	Rustic
Time	3 hours

The trail climbs very steeply at first before leveling out. You soon cross Mountain Highway on your way. There are several places where the trail cuts into Skyline Drive, though the main trail actually runs above it. If you get onto Skyline, either retrace your steps to see where you left the trail, or just climb Skyline to where the trail picks up again, west of one of the curves. The old chairlift used to take off from the end of Skyline Drive.

How To Get There

From the Trans-Canada Highway (#1) in either direction take exit #19 (Lynn Valley Road) and follow Lynn Valley Road northeast to where it seems to turn left onto Dempsey. Keep going straight. The trailhead is almost all the way up the access road (to **Lynn Headwaters Regional Park**).

Or, park at Lynn Valley Road and Dempsey and walk in on the **Rice Lake Road Trail**.

Hero's Rating: 🐾 🐾   **Human's Rating:** ★ ★ ★ ★

Skyline to Grouse Mt. Gondola Parking Lot

Park Number	50
Trail Difficulty	3 - 4
Trail Condition	Rustic
Time	3 hours

The trail access is almost at the top of Skyline Drive, which is where the old Grouse chairlift platform used to be. The trail skirts the edge of a steep mountainside, scrambles over a few creeks (which could well be impassable when in flood) and then past the sight of the infamous Grouse Grind before entering the east end of the Grouse Mountain Gondola parking lot. Unfortunately the people who run Grouse Mountain no longer allow dogs on the gondola nor the part of the mountain which they own.

A nice way to return on this walk is to come back on the **Powerlines Trail** (just look up and find the powerlines, you can't miss them). You then have to climb Skyline Drive back up to your car, or, there are a few parking spots right at the powerlines, and you can start your hike with a walk up Skyline when you are fresh. To get from the parking lot to Cleveland Dam you have to walk down Nancy Green Way, a road lined with houses.

How To Get There

From downtown Vancouver take Georgia Street to the Lions Gate Bridge. Take the North Vancouver off-ramp (right). Then turn left on Capilano Road, the first intersection after the bridge.

From the Trans-Canada Highway (#1) in either direction take exit #14 (Capilano Road).

Follow Capilano Road north to Montroyal. Turn Right (east) on Montroyal. Skyline goes north (up) from here. Follow Skyline to the top.

Or, follow Capilano Road north to its end. The Baden-Powell is accessed off the east side of the lot, but so are several other trails so mind the signage. The **Powerlines** that you can see are not the Baden-Powell.

Hero's Rating: 🐾 🐾   **Human's Rating:** ★ ★ ★ ★

Cleveland Dam to Glenmore

Park Number	50
Trail Difficulty	3 - 4
Trail Condition	Good
Time	1 hour

The Cleveland Dam is a great place for just staring at the tons of water rushing down the spillway. Crossing the Cleveland Dam, take the higher of two roads that fork to the left. This climbs through a small section of forest to a road in the British Properties. If you like this hike, try the rest of **Capilano Canyon**.

How To Get There

From downtown Vancouver take Georgia Street to the Lions Gate Bridge. Take the North Vancouver off-ramp (right). Then turn left on Capilano Road, the first intersection after the bridge.

From the Trans-Canada Highway (#1) in either direction take exit #14 (Capilano Road).

Follow Capilano Road north. The Cleveland Dam parking lot is on your left across from the Canyon Gardens Chinese Restaurant, which has been in that location for many, many years.

Hero's Rating: 🐾 🐾   **Human's Rating:** ★ ★ ★

Baden-Powell West

For the continuance of the Baden-Powell see under this heading in West Vancouver.

Bridle Path

Park Number	51
Trail Difficulty	3 - 4
Trail Condition	Rustic
Time	2 - 3 hours

A semiwilderness walk through dense evergreen forests. The trails in this area are many and they crisscross each other in a confusing way so be careful, take a compass, and give yourself lots of time. Sometimes this trail joins the **Baden-Powell**, sometimes it crosses it, sometimes it is the same trail as the Pipeline Road in **Northlands**.

There was no sign of horses on the trail the day I hiked it, and it's an awfully rough, rocky, overgrown trail for horses to travel, but keep on the watch for them nonetheless. What you will see are lots of mountain bikers.

Near the east end of this trail there is an upper loop that climbs to a lookout where you can see the Indian Arm and Burnaby Mountain. The golf course has taken over most of the southeast section of the trail, so the Parks Board has been revising the **Old Buck Trail** (see **Mount Seymour Provincial Park**) to take it the last leg of the way to Mount Seymour Road.

How To Get There

From the Trans-Canada Highway (#1) take exit #22. If you have been traveling eastbound take the overpass left across the highway.

Near the Superstore, turn right onto Mount Seymour Parkway, then take the Parkway to Mount Seymour Road. Turn left.

You can access this trail from the parking lot at the bottom of Mount Seymour. Just walk a little way up Mount Seymour Road to where the **Old Buck** trail starts on the left.

You can access the west end of the trail off Riverside Drive, (watch for parking restrictions in the summer) or from many roads in Lynn Valley that reach the treeline, or from inside the **Seymour Demonstration Forest**.

Hero's Rating: 🐾 🐾   **Human's Rating:** ★ ★ ★

Capilano River Regional Park

Park Number	52
Trail Difficulty	1 - 5
Trail Condition	Excellent to fair
Time	Endless

This park contains the Cleveland Dam, splendid, huge old trees, a salmon hatchery, spectacular canyons, a Commuter Cycling Trail, and, of course, the Capilano River. These beautiful evergreen forests contain 26 km of trails, one of which leaves the park and goes all the way down to **Ambleside Beach**. Those trails that pass by the hatchery and the dam will be very busy with tourists in the summer months. Handicap access is limited to the Cleveland Dam area and the Hatchery itself.

WARNING: The river current can be very strong. See **About Rivers** in the Trail Wisdom section of the book.

Water quality in the Capilano River is Good.

How To Get There

From downtown Vancouver take Georgia Street to the Lions Gate Bridge. Take the North Vancouver off-ramp (right). Turn left on Capilano Road, the first intersection after the bridge.

From the Trans-Canada Highway (#1) take the Capilano Road / Grouse Mountain exit (#14).

Drive north (toward the mountain) on Capilano Road to the Fish Hatchery turnoff, (just past the Capilano Suspension Bridge) or continue to the Cleveland Dam parking lot.

Commuter Cycling Trail

Park Number	52
Trail Difficulty	3
Trail Condition	Good
Time	1 hour

Runs west from the Cleveland Dam through to West Vancouver along the graveled service road.

Hero's Rating: 🐾   **Human's Rating:** ★

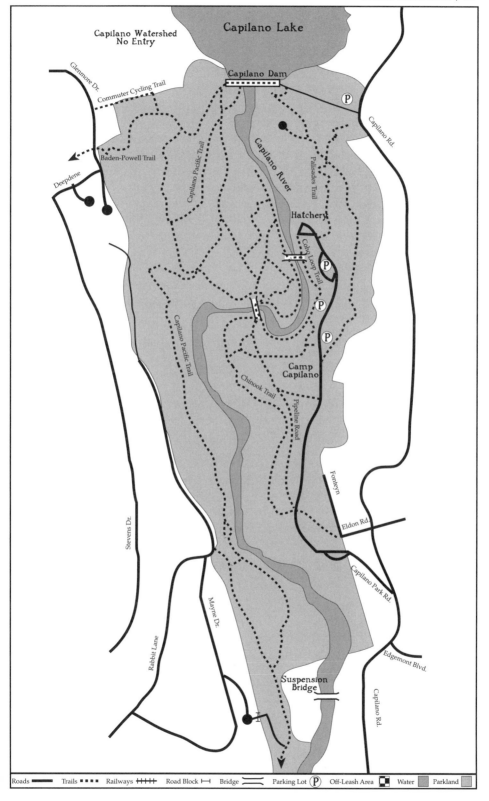

Roads ▬▬▬ Trails ▪▪▪▪ Railways ┼┼┼┼ Road Block ┠─┨ Bridge ═══ Parking Lot Ⓟ Off-Leash Area ⬛ Water ◻ Parkland ▨

Capilano Pacific Trail

Park Number	52
Trail Difficulty	2
Trail Condition	Excellent to good
Time	4 - 5 hours

Runs all the way from the Cleveland Dam at the top of the park, down the west bank to **Ambleside Beach** at the mouth of the River. The first part winds downstream through the park with a few places where you can get down to the river, though often there are anglers down there who glare coldly at dogs and their owners. Again, please exercise caution. You end up on a road that takes you past Woodbine, a development of high-rise condos. Watch for the signs that will direct you back to the river. The second part of the trail is highly groomed with many easy access points to the river, which is much shallower here. The trail leaves the river, and cuts through the driveway of a long-term care facility before cutting behind the Park Royal Hotel and then the parking lot of the Mall. Stay to your left and the trail will cut into the woods, taking you under the train tracks to **Ambleside Beach** .

Hero's Rating: 🐾 🐾 🐾 🐾   **Human's Rating:** ★ ★ ★ ★

Chinook Trail

Park Number	52
Trail Difficulty	2 - 3
Trail Condition	Fair
Time	1 - 2 hour s

This trail is bit more off the beaten track and the park has some flatish areas. It goes through a really nice forest of tall straight firs, ending up where the Pipeline Road meets the paved access road. You can take the Pipeline Road back to make a nice loop.

Hero's Rating: 🐾 🐾 🐾 🐾   **Human's Rating:** ★ ★ ★ ★

Coho Loop Trail

Park Number	52
Trail Difficulty	3
Trail Condition	Good
Time	45 minutes

From the bridge at the hatchery you can go down either side of the river to the old pipe bridge perched high above the water, and walk back up the other side. This trail will be very, very busy during tourist season.

Hero's Rating: 🐾 🐾 🐾 🐾   **Human's Rating:** ★ ★ ★ ★

Palisades Trail

Park Number	52
Trail Difficulty	3
Trail Condition	Fair
Time	30 minutes

Runs down the east bank of the river from the Dam to the hatchery. Look for the trailhead just before you get to the actual dam structure.

Hero's Rating: 🐾 🐾   **Human's Rating:** ★ ★

Pipeline Road

Park Number	52
Trail Difficulty	3
Trail Condition	Good
Time	45 minutes

This is an old access road for the pipe that forms the pipe bridge, which hangs high above the canyon bottom. Quite spectacular and not to be missed.

Hero's Rating: 🐾 🐾 🐾   **Human's Rating:** ★ ★ ★ ★

Shinglebolt Trails

Park Number	52
Trail Difficulty	3 - 4
Trail Condition	Fair
Time	1 - 2 hours

In a fairly remote section, these trails offer a bit of climbing without so many people.

Hero's Rating: 🐾 🐾 🐾   **Human's Rating:** ★ ★ ★

Cates Park

Park Number	53
Trail Difficulty	1
Trail Condition	Excellent
Time	30 minutes

Cates Park is largely off-limits to your dog. At the far east side of the parking lot, however, is the Malcolm Lowry Walk. Lowry was the author of the classic *Under the Volcano*, and was booted out of a squatter's shack situated along this walk, that was subsequently, ironically, named after him. And so it goes.

The trail stays close by the shore, with many small beaches long the way. Eventually you reach Little Cates Park, another playground from which your dog is prohibited. There are a few more trails between the two parks and above the Malcolm Lowry Walk. Great views across Indian Arm.

Water Quality in Indian Arm is Fair.

How To Get There

Heading west on the Trans-Canada Highway (#1) take the very first exit (#23B) off the Second Narrows Bridge. This is Main Street which turns into the old Dollarton Highway. Take the Dollarton east almost to Deep Cove. The park is to the right of the road and is well marked.

Hero's Rating: 🐾 🐾   **Human's Rating:** ★ ★

The Grouse Grind

Park Number	54
Trail Difficulty	4 - 5
Trail Condition	Rustic
Time	30 minutes

The Grouse Grind is a very well known North Shore hike due to some media events which are sponsored here. This is one of the less attractive hikes on the North Shore, traveling right under the gondola. Dogs are not allowed at the top of the mountain. If you want a good steep hike try the **Old Grouse Trail**. Much prettier and with a nicer destination.

How To Get There

From downtown Vancouver take Georgia Street to the Lions Gate Bridge. Take the North Vancouver off-ramp (right). Turn left on Capilano Road, the first intersection after the bridge.

From the Trans-Canada Highway (#1) in either direction take exit #14 (Capilano Road).

Follow Capilano Road north to its end. The Grouse Grind is accessed off the Baden-Powell, which is accessed off the east side of the Grouse Mountain parking lot, but so are several other trails, so mind the signage.

Hero's Rating: No Paws   **Human's Rating: No Stars**

Harbourview Park

Park Number	55
Trail Difficulty	1
Trail Condition	Excellent
Time	20 minutes

A short jaunt beside the dockyard down to the very mouth of Lynn Creek. The trail follows close by the creek to the harbour where there is a raised viewing platform from which you can look out over the harbour and the dock there. I love to watch other people work, don't you? There is a ramp to this platform, making it wheelchair accessible. Wonderful views across the harbour to the south shore. Interesting tugboat and dock activity. Good water access for Hero.

Water quality in Vancouver Harbour is Fair.

How To Get There

Heading west on the Trans-Canada Highway (#1) take the second exit (#23A) off the Second Narrows Bridge. This will get you onto Main going west. Turn left (south) on Mountain Highway, proceed two blocks south of Main Street to Dominion Street. Turn right. Proceed to Harbour Avenue, turn right again and then left onto a dirt road that will take you to the parking lot.

Hero's Rating: 🐾 🐾   **Human's Rating:** ★ ★

Hastings Creek Trail

Park Number	56
Trail Difficulty	2
Trail Condition	Good
Time	1 hour

A creek park surrounded by housing. This trail will be attractive mainly to locals or those who want a short walk in the woods of less than one hour duration. Houses line the left bank for part of the way as you progress up stream on the right bank. The trail terminates at a schoolyard. The creek is fairly clean for a suburban creek.

How To Get There

From the Trans-Canada Highway (#1) take the Mountain Highway exit (#21) to Arborlynn, which bears off to the right. Arborlynn becomes Hoskins. There is parking immediately on your left. Alternately you can access it off Poplynn and 21st, or Allan, a small cul-de-sac off Ross Road.

Hero's Rating: 🐾   **Human's Rating:** ★

Indian River Drive

Park Number	57
Trail Difficulty	2 - 4
Trail Condition	Excellent
Time	4 - 5 hours

This road is designated as an Off-Leash Area. I'm not sure I'd want to walk it, however, as there is no actual trail. You are walking on the road itself, which, though not a busy road, is so narrow that in places only one car at a time can pass through. It might be fun to cycle, but I'd still be very leery of traffic and only do this with a well-trained, very traffic-savvy dog.

At the end of the road is a small community called Woodlands nestled on the west bank of the Indian Arm, a long fjord that branches off from Burrard Inlet. There is a government wharf there and very little else. There is virtually no parking.

How To Get There

From the Trans-Canada Highway (#1) take exit # 22. If you have been traveling eastbound take the left to the overpass across the highway.

Near the Superstore, turn right onto Mount Seymour Parkway. Turn left on Mount Seymour Road (the road that goes up the mountain to the ski area). Before you actually head up the hill, there is a turnoff to the right; this is Indian River Road. Indian River Road goes through a new subdivision with a school (watch your speed) before joining up with the old road.

Hero's Rating: 🐾 🐾   **Human's Rating: ★ ★**

Lillooet Road

Park Number	58
Trail Difficulty	2
Trail Condition	Good
Time	1 - 2 hours

A gravel road that leads from behind Capilano College to Rice Lake and the **Seymour Demonstration Forest**. Very dusty on a hot dry day, but a great place to bike with your dog just the same. There is a trail on a berm; a raised bank on the east side of the road that keeps you away from the traffic.

How To Get There

From the Trans-Canada Highway (#1) take exit #22. If you have been traveling eastbound go left across the overpass. Proceed straight through the lights, up the hill, past Capilano College, and the graveyard. Lillooet Road continues as the dirt road that goes from the graveyard to the Rice Lake parking lot.

Hero's Rating: 🐾   **Human's Rating: ★**

Loutet Park

Park Number	59
Trail Difficulty	2 - 3
Trail Condition	Rustic
Time	1 hour

Loutet Park itself is a playing field, but there is a trail that runs through the woods behind (east of) the park and south down the "Cut" on the highway to Keith Road. It also returns (northwest) through the forest toward Sutherland school, coming out on 18th and Williams.

How To Get There
Access trail at Keith and Brooksbank, 18th and Williams, or behind (east of) Loutet Park, on Rufus, three blocks east of Grand Boulevard, between 17th and 13th.

Hero's Rating: ❧   **Human's Rating:** ★

Lynn Canyon Park

Park Number	60
Trail Difficulty	1 - 5
Trail Condition	Good to Rustic
Time	Endless

Fishing | Biking | Drinking | Phone | Off-Leash
Horses | Jogging | Access | Washroom | Water | Prohibited

The park straddles Lynn Creek from the Trans-Canada Highway up to the Canyon Park proper with its suspension bridge. **Lynn Headwaters Regional Park** is just above and **Seymour Demonstration Forest** shares most of its east boundary. This park sports old growth forest and a deep canyon with the clear green waters of Lynn Creek. The Suspension Bridge is not to be missed. It spans the canyon at a point where the drop exceeds 50 metres.

There are a few small trails on the western side, with steps to the bridge over Twin Falls, but the main attractions are the Lower Lynn Trail and Middle Lynn Trails, that lead to the east bank all the way downstream to the highway.

A 10-minute walk upstream on the east side from the suspension bridge brings you to the 30-Foot Pool, a lovely place. If you climb the stairs above the pool, you can connect to trails that lead into the Seymour Demonstration Forest, but Lynn Headwaters Park lies beyond a no-dog zone on the east side. To get to Lynn Headwaters Park from here you would have to cross back over to the west side and follow the **Rice Lake Road Trail** (see **Baden-Powell Trail**).

WARNING: The canyon walls are steep and unsafe. Exercise caution and stay on the paths. The river current can be very strong. See **About Rivers** in the Trail Wisdom section of the book.

Water quality in Lynn Creek is Good.

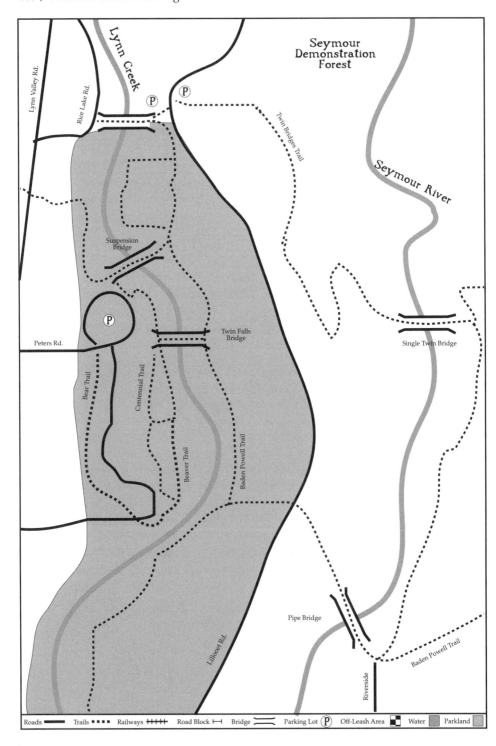

How To Get There

From the Trans-Canada Highway (#1) in either direction take exit #19 (Lynn Valley Road) and follow Lynn Valley Road northeast. Watch for a sign on the right side of the road. Follow the signs (Peters Road) to the parking lot.

Park Drive

Park Number	60
Trail Difficulty	1
Trail Condition	Good
Time	30 minutes

The Park Drive is zoned Off-Leash between Ross Road and the Lynn Canyon Park picnic area.

Hero's Rating: 🐾 🐾   **Human's Rating:** ★ ★

Lynn Creek Trail (Lower)

Park Number	60
Trail Difficulty	1
Trail Condition	Good
Time	30 minutes - 1 hour

An open walk on wide roads beside Lynn Creek, this whole trail is zoned Off-Leash. From Bridgman Park the trail goes up the west side of the creek and crosses over a pedestrian bridge, that cyclists use from Capilano College through to Lynn Valley. You can also start from Seylynn Park, across the creek from Bridgman Park.

All along this road are access points to the creek, which is quite clean, but most people wait until after the pedestrian bridge to follow their dogs down to the banks and sit by the water. At a certain point this road turns right and heads into a barren dumping ground. If you go straight however, you connect to the Middle Lynn Trail.

Hero loves the water access here, and he loves all the social interaction. Expect to meet many other canines here on a typical day, including a group that walks the SPCA's current inmates. There are some nice places to sit on the rocks by the creek, and in the summer you can even swim here.

WARNING: The river current can be very strong. See **About Rivers** in the Trail Wisdom section of the book.

Water quality in Lynn Creek is Good.

How To Get There
East side

From the Trans-Canada Highway (#1) take exit #22. If you have been traveling eastbound take the left to the overpass across the highway.

Take an immediate left at the lights, in front of the CoachHouse Inn. Take the right after the CoachHouse (otherwise you'll go back onto the highway). Turn a shallow left on Premier. When the houses end, turn left toward the sports field.

West side

At the bottom of the hill on Keith Road, going east toward the highway, turn right into the parking lot for Bridgman Park. Ignore the No Dogs signs and drive past the kiddie playground to which they pertain and park at the turnaround. The trail starts here and goes directly under the highway on the west side of the creek.

Hero's Rating: 🐾 🐾 🐾 🐾 🐾   **Human's Rating:** ★ ★ ★ ★

Lynn Creek Trail (Middle)

Park Number	60
Trail Difficulty	3 - 4
Trail Condition	Rustic
Time	2 hours

Off-Leash

Water

Middle Lynn is a lovely trail through a beautiful forest, and dips down to the water several times. It's a nice aerobic climb through the forest and meets with the **Baden-Powell Trail**, **Seymour Demonstration Forest**, and **Lynn Headwaters**. You will come to a bridge that crosses over the river by a double falls; this is Twin Falls Bridge, and somewhere here the off-leash zoning ends. The second bridge you will come to is the famous suspension bridge. In the summer, watch for hordes of tourists once you reach this area.

WARNING: The river current can be very strong. See **About Rivers** in the Trail Wisdom section of the book.

Water quality in Lynn Creek is Good.

How To Get There

Follow directions to **Lower Lynn Trail** to access from the bottom of the trail, or follow directions to **Lynn Canyon Park** to access from the top.

Hero's Rating: 🐾 🐾 🐾 🐾 🐾   **Human's Rating:** ★ ★ ★ ★ ★

Lynn Headwaters Regional Park

Park Number	61
Trail Difficulty	1 - 5
Trail Condition	Good to rustic
Time	Endless

Fishing | Drinking | Phone

Jogging | Access | Washroom | Water

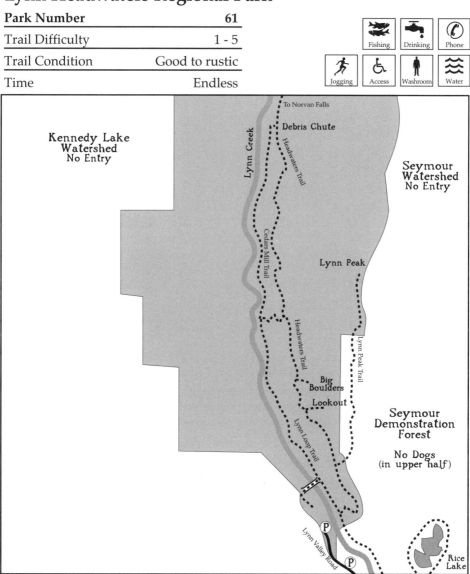

One of the wilder walks in the Lower Mainland, **Lynn Headwaters is** connected to the **Baden-Powell Trail, Seymour Demonstration Forest**, and **Lynn Canyon Park**. There are washrooms and a phone by the parking lot, then you're on your own.

The extensive park trails follow Lynn Creek (which is as large as most rivers) up the steep valley. Way up the valley there is the lovely Norvan Falls, or if you are up for a bit of a climb, then Lynn Peak provides a view to the east.

WARNING: The river current can be very strong. See **About Rivers** in the Trail Wisdom section of the book.

Water quality in Lynn Creek is Good.

How To Get There

From the Trans-Canada Highway (#1) in either direction take exit #19 (Lynn Valley Road) and follow Lynn Valley Road northeast to where it seems to turn left at Dempsey. Keep going straight through this intersection and along the access road (still actually called Lynn Valley Road) to the parking lots.

You can't walk directly through the Seymour Demonstration Forest to get to Lynn Headwaters with your dog, because dogs aren't allowed above the Rice Lake Parking lot. What you have to do is cross the bridge at Rice Lake Road, just to the west of the parking lot, then take the **Rice Lake Road Trail**, or walk up Lynn Valley Road to the Headwaters. From Lynn Canyon you can take the **Baden-Powell Trail** up the west bank to where it emerges at Lynn Valley Road and Dempsey, then go down Rice Lake Road Trail as well.

Cedars Mill Trail

Park Number	61
Trail Difficulty	1
Trail Condition	Good
Time	1 hour

Where Lynn Loop turns back this trail continues along the creek and connects with the Headwaters Trail, that climbs into the woods, paralleling the Cedar Mill Trail back to the Lynn Loop Trail, or carries on to Norvan Falls. Look for logging paraphernalia along this trail.

Hero's Rating: 🐾 🐾 🐾 🐾   **Human's Rating:** ★ ★ ★ ★

Headwaters Trail

Park Number	61
Trail Difficulty	3
Trail Condition	Rustic
Time	2 - 3 hours

This trail begins where Lynn Loop trail turns back. The trail parallels the Cedar Mill Trail (which runs beside the river) but up the mountainside. When Cedar Mill Trail runs out, Headwaters Trail continues up to Norvan Falls. There are a few really lovely views of the valley on this walk. Even in the pouring rain this park is beautiful, when clouds wreathe the mountains in mystery.

Hero's Rating: 🐾 🐾 🐾   **Human's Rating:** ★ ★ ★ ★

Lynn Loop Trail

Park Number	61
Trail Difficulty	2
Trail Condition	Rustic
Time	2 - 3 hours

The Lynn Loop Trail is what you start on however you begin. It follows the east side of the creek, with plenty of opportunities to dabble your paws, until it meets the Cedars Mill Trail, then cuts up the side of the mountain to meet with the beginning of the Headwaters Trail before turning back. Off the upper part of the Lynn Loop Trail there are several trails leading up the mountain. One will take you to Lynn Peak.

Hero's Rating: 🐾 🐾 🐾 🐾   **Human's Rating: ★ ★ ★ ★**

Lynn Peak Trail

Park Number	61
Trail Difficulty	4
Trail Condition	Rustic
Time	3 - 4 hours

You will have to hike a very steep trail to get to the view, but it is worth it. It's about 2.5 km from where it leaves the upper part of the Lynn Loop Trail. And what a view. Great cardio workout here. And did I mention the view?

Hero's Rating: 🐾 🐾 🐾   **Human's Rating: ★ ★ ★ ★**

Norvan Falls Trail

Park Number	61
Trail Difficulty	3
Trail Condition	Fair
Time	3 - 4 hours

This trail starts where the Mill Creek and Headwaters Trails meet at their far end. The falls are quite lovely and you can sit on the rocks in a fine mist and eat lunch. If you are really intrepid, and well prepared to travel tough, extremely rustic paths, you can go past the falls on very rough trails, 6 km to Crown Pass, and along the alpine trail, eventually getting all the way to Grouse Mountain. Unfortunately Grouse Mountain does not allow dogs on their property. Otherwise you could take the tram down to Grouse Mountain Road.

Hero's Rating: 🐾 🐾 🐾 🐾   **Human's Rating: ★ ★ ★ ★ ★**

MacKay Creek

Park Number	62
Trail Difficulty	1 - 3
Trail Condition	Good to poor
Time	Endless

MacKay Creek runs through several parks on its way down the mountain. I grew up along this creek, on the section just above Heywood Park, and I realized as I walked here, just a couple of days after my 40th birthday (gad), that I had come full circle in a sense. Here I was, doing what I had spent most of my free time doing all those years ago; mucking about down the creek with my dog.

MacKay Creek Park

Park Number	62
Trail Difficulty	1 - 3
Trail Condition	Poor
Time	30 minutes

Just south of Handsworth School, off Edgewood, there is a footbridge crossing the creek. Deer trails run down from here on either side of the creek, sometimes following old creek beds. A bit of a scramble, but a nice creek with lots of cool pools for a dog to dip into.

There are a couple of walkable sections higher up the creek, above Montroyal, but they are segmented by roads.

Hero's Rating: 🐾 🐾 🐾   **Human's Rating:** ★ ★ ★

Murdo Fraser Park

Park Number	62
Trail Difficulty	1 - 3
Trail Condition	Good
Time	10 minutes

There is a trail on the creek just below Edgemont Village. This takes you past a pond that dogs are restricted from, and on to Murdo Fraser Park where there are tennis courts and a kiddie playground.

How To Get There

Access at Murdo Fraser Park or from Crescentview Drive off Edgemont Boulevard.

Hero's Rating: 🐾   **Human's Rating:** ★

Heywood Park

Park Number	62
Trail Difficulty	1 - 2
Trail Condition	Poor
Time	30 minutes - 1 hour

Although there is a park with a playground right at Marine Drive, for our purposes this is a linear creek park with housing on either side. Several trails run up MacKay creek from Heywood Park, one on either side close to the creek and one higher up the bank on the east side. The high road will take you from Hamilton Street near the park to the old Hamilton Jr. Secondary School, now an adult education centre. To head back downstream, you can access the lower trail just before the complex, or you can go to the northwest corner of the fields and access a trail that goes through to Pemberton Heights, passing over a bridge and coming out at MacKay Avenue and 23rd. The lower trails above the bridge are basically deer trails and peter out at the highway.

On the lower trails, be wary of several dilapidated bridges, mossy stumps, and slippery mud.

How To Get There

Take Marine Drive to MacKay or Hamilton. Heywood Park is on Marine between MacKay and Hamilton.

Hero's Rating: 🐾 🐾   **Human's Rating:** ★ ★

Mahon Park

Park Number	63
Trail Difficulty	1 - 2
Trail Condition	Good
Time	30 minutes

A linear creek park for our purposes, Mahon Park includes a large, gravel track field (this is where they hold the annual Fireman's Hose Reel) and a grass soccer field where Kinsman Stadium used to be before it was burned down. In between these two fields there are a few trails that follow the creek down a ravine, meet at the bottom, and make a nice circuit for a half-hour walk. Just down the trail from a small baseball diamond behind the soccer field is a small clearing or meadow where we used to go hang out when we went to Carson Graham School. The creek is not very clean, however.

How To Get There

The trails in Mahon can be accessed at Jones and 18th or on the north side of W. 13th Street, just east of Bewicke.

Hero's Rating: 🐾 🐾 🐾   **Human's Rating:** ★ ★

Maplewood Flats Wildlife Sanctuary

Park Number	64
Trail Difficulty	1
Trail Condition	Good
Time	15 minutes

A shoreside park on a muddy bay. This park was going to be turned into condos or industry until the Wild Bird Trust of BC lobbied to have it set aside. They only allow dogs on the east side of the park, which means the walk you can do with a dog is a bit short, and because the area is environmentally sensitive, you really must keep the dog on leash. The shore is so muddy I'm not sure you'd want your dog to run free there anyway.

Water quality in Burrard Inlet here is Fair.

How To Get There

Heading west on the Trans-Canada Highway (#1) take the very first exit (#23B) off the Second Narrows Bridge. This is Main Street which turns into the old Dollarton Highway.

Take the Dollarton Highway east. Watch for the Pacific Environmental Science Centre. The park is accessed off the end of this parking lot.

Hero's Rating: 🐾   **Human's Rating:** ★

Mosquito Creek

Park Number	65
Trail Difficulty	1 - 2
Trail Condition	Excellent
Time	2 hours

A linear creek park with housing on either side. Mosquito Creek Trail follows the creek up from the kiddie park on Larson and Fell all the way to Mount Royal, and past, if you are intrepid, to meet with the **Baden-Powell Trail**. The main trail is west of the creek and wide enough in most parts to drive a truck down (though it is off-limits to vehicles, of course). The lower part is bowered by trees and the upper (above Queens) is open to the elements. When you get to William Griffin Park on Queens, where there is a community centre, you must cross the road and go up Del Rio street to its end and the trail will pick up again.

How To Get There

You can access this trail from the park at Fell and Larson, just north of Marine Drive, or from just above William Griffin Park on Queens (take Del Rio), or from the top on Mount Royal, where the firehall is.

Hero's Rating: 🐾 🐾 🐾   **Human's Rating:** ★ ★ ★

Mount Seymour Provincial Park

Park Number	66
Trail Difficulty	1 - 5
Trail Condition	Good to rustic
Time	Endless

Biking | Drinking | Phone

Washroom | Water | Prohibited

Roads ▬ Trails ▪▪▪▪ Railways ┼┼┼┼ Road Block ⊢⊣ Bridge ⤳ Parking Lot Ⓟ Off-Leash Area ▦ Water ▨ Parkland ▨

Mount Seymour Park is in a wilderness area. This means you must be prepared for all that entails. See Trail Wisdom in the General section of the book. There are washrooms, a phone, and drinking water by the parking lot.

There are many, many trails in this park, so I will outline a couple of the better ones for dogs. If you want to further explore this area, pamphlets are available from BC Parks (see appendix).

How To Get There

From the Trans-Canada Highway (#1) take exit #22. If you have been traveling eastbound take the left to the overpass across the highway.

Near the Superstore, turn right onto Mount Seymour Parkway. Turn left on

Mount Seymour Road. The drive to the top takes about 15 minutes or so. Goldie and Flower Lakes Loops and Dog Mountain Trail leave from this parking lot.

Dog Mountain Trail

Park Number	66
Trail Difficulty	3
Trail Condition	Rustic
Time	1 - 2 hours

With a name like this, you'd expect that dogs would be welcome off-leash. Such is not the case, however.

The trip to Dog Mountain starts at the upper end of the parking lot at the top of the road. There is signage that will direct you to the trail. The trail climbs up and down clefts in the mountain and is very muddy, so you should have good waterproof shoes for this one. In early fall the trail becomes icy and can be quite treacherous. Even in summer the trail is bumpy with roots and rocks, so great care is necessary.

At the end of the trail you will climb onto a rocky bluff that looks out onto Greater Vancouver and the Fraser Valley. On a clear day you can see Vancouver Island and down the coast into the USA.

For the extremely adventurous, there is a way you can make a circle from Dog Mountain, rather than going back on the same trail. Right at the bottom of the rocky bluff, you turn left. This takes you along the Suicide Bluffs, however, and is not for the faint hearted. This trail has a Difficulty Rating of 5 or maybe 6! There is some actual climbing involved and the terrain rises and falls steeply for its entirety. It is marked only by red tags on the trees, so I only recommend this trail for very experienced hikers in good shape. Be aware that you will have to haul your dog up some steep rocky bits by his collar. Hero actually enjoyed this! Eventually this trail will get you back to a ski run.

Hero's Rating: 🐾 🐾   **Human's Rating:** ★ ★ ★

Mystery Lake Trail

Park Number	66
Trail Difficulty	3 - 4
Trail Condition	Good
Time	1 - 2 hours

Another popular summer trail, it climbs under the chairlift to Mystery Lake, a nice place for a swim on a hot day, especially after hiking up there.

Hero's Rating: 🐾 🐾 🐾   **Human's Rating:** ★ ★ ★ ★

Goldie and Flower Lake Loop Trails

Park Number	66
Trail Difficulty	2 - 3
Trail Condition	Good
Time	1 - 2 hours

Water

Although these trails get kinda crowded in the summer time, they are still worth checking out. Trails goes through subalpine bog dotted with ponds and small lakes. The hike to Goldie is very easy, while you have to do a bit of climbing to get to Flower Lake.

Hero's Rating: 🐾 🐾 🐾　　　　**Human's Rating:** ★ ★ ★ ★

The Old Buck Trail

Park Number	66
Trail Difficulty	3 - 4
Trail Condition	Rustic
Time	2 - 4 hours

The Old Buck Logging Trail, as it is also known, climbs rather steeply into Mount Seymour Provincial Park to meet with the **Baden-Powell** (about 1 hour), then with the Perimeter Trail another 2 hours or so up the trail.

The Old Buck Trail has a high rocky bluff about 15 minutes up the trail that looks over across Deep Cove and Indian Arm to **Belcarra Regional Park** in Burnaby.

In recent years the Old Buck has been getting a bit overgrown, but I noticed some work going on there recently so I think it may have been cleared some.

Update: I went back to check on the trail and boy has it changed! There is now a clear trailhead and the trail has been groomed and cleared. There is now a layer of fresh gravel on the path and new directional signposts with maps of the area and "you are here" markers. Thanks, BC Parks!

How To Get There
You can access this trail from the parking lot at the bottom of Mount Seymour Road. The first trailhead is just on the west side of the road, right where Indian River Road connects to the east.

This will take you a ways up Mount Seymour Road, where, at the access to the new golf course (Anne MacDonald Way) there is a serious trailhead with a small parking lot, a bulletin board, and an outhouse.

Hero's Rating: 🐾 🐾　　　　**Human's Rating:** ★ ★ ★

Mountain Highway

Park Number	67
Trail Difficulty	3
Trail Condition	Good
Time	3 - 5 hours

It is possible to walk (or bike or cross-country ski) up Mountain Highway after the paved road ends, where it is also known as Grouse Mountain Road, because that's where it ends up. It's a bit of a long haul, but there is a view at the top, and you can follow the road quite far up the mountain. The road takes you to the same place as the **Old Grouse Trail,** which is much steeper but a nicer hike.

How To Get There

From the Trans-Canada Highway (#1) take exit #21 north. Follow Mountain Highway to a gate.

Hero's Rating: 🐾 🐾   **Human's Rating:** ★ ★

Northlands

Park Number	68
Trail Difficulty	2
Trail Condition	Fair
Time	1 hour

Recently the North Shore residents scored a victory over the CMHC, who wanted to develop this area for housing. The area has been temporarily saved by rezoning it, but not from other types of possible future development. Stay tuned.

Meanwhile, Northlands is an area that used to be the Blair Rifle Range, where they taught guys to shoot during the war. Delineated by Mount Seymour Parkway to the south and by housing on either side, it is riddled with a confusing array of old roads and covered with a young forest of alder. Watch for broken glass, as partiers have used this site for years.

Off-Leash Area

At the top of the Northlands area is the Pipeline Road, designated Off-Leash, which runs east-west and now (since the building of the new golf course) seems to have been amalgamated with the **Bridle Path.**

How To Get There

Access off Mount Seymour Parkway between Berkley and Mount Seymour Road. Or, take Mount Seymour Parkway to Berkley to Hyannis. Access at the end of Hill Drive off Hyannis, or the end of Dresden Way; small feeder trails will take you there. The main entrance to the Pipeline Road is off Tompkins Crescent.

Access the east end of the trail at Mount Seymour Road.

Hero's Rating: 🐾 🐾 🐾   **Human's Rating:** ★ ★

Old Grouse Trail

Park Number	69
Trail Difficulty	4 - 5
Trail Condition	Poor
Time	2 - 3 hours

A very steep and unmaintained trail, the Old Grouse Trail leaves from close to where the **Baden-Powell Trail** crosses **Mosquito Creek Trail** by the water towers. Take the **Baden-Powell** to the east and very shortly you will see a marker that says Old Grouse Mountain Highway.

The trail cuts pretty well straight up the mountain to arrive at **Mountain Highway**, a gravel road. If you follow this road you will eventually get to Grouse Mountain. There used to be quite a view from the road, but now the trees have grown up so that you only get a peek.

Careful on this trail if you go in the snow. Icy snow over jagged rocks makes for a nasty trail on which to fall.

The water noted above is the Mosquito Creek. There are also a few smaller creeks on this walk.

How To Get There

Take the Trans-Canada Highway (#1) to Lonsdale (exit #18). Go north up Lonsdale to the top, where the road turns to the left, then right onto Prospect. The Old Grouse Trail is accessed at the top of Prospect Road.

Hero's Rating: 🐾 🐾   **Human's Rating:** ★ ★ ★

Other Off-Leash Areas

There are additional minor areas that have been designated Off-Leash by the district of North Vancouver. The city of North Vancouver has no Off-Leash Areas as of yet.

Cap Powerlines

Park Number	n/a
Trail Difficulty	2 - 3
Trail Condition	Fair
Time	15 minutes

Below the condos by Capilano College there are a number of paths running through the bushes under the powerlines. I kept this out of the Powerlines heading because it's so different, being a small square park rather than a long linear one.

How To Get There

It's bordered on the west by Lillooet Road, which goes up to the college, and by what eventually turns into Mount Seymour Parkway on the south.

Hero's Rating: 🐾 🐾   **Human's Rating:** ★

The Cut

Park Number	n/a
Trail Difficulty	2 - 3
Trail Condition	Poor
Time	30 minutes

A trail follows the Trans-Canada Highway (#1) down the east side of "The Cut." The trail is unkempt and sandwiched between the highway and the yards above.

How To Get There

Access from Casano Road in Lynn Valley.

Hero's Rating: 🐾   **Human's Rating: No Stars**

Hunter Park

Park Number	n/a
Trail Difficulty	1
Trail Condition	Excellent
Time	15 minutes

Just below **Princess Park** is an area some maps call Hunter Park. There is a nice, flat gravel path here that runs beside a creek between houses and a little pond where the kids seem to swim in the summer (there's a small raft floating in the middle). If you follow the creek up a deer trail (the difficulty rating would be about a 3 on a very rustic trail) you can get to the powerlines that meet up with **Princess Park.**

How To Get There

You can access this trail from Williams or Tennyson or Chaucer.

Hero's Rating: 🐾 🐾   **Human's Rating:** ★ ★

Malaspina Park

Park Number	n/a
Trail Difficulty	3 - 4
Trail Condition	Fair
Time	15 minutes

Just above Malaspina Place the trees begin. This area is apparently the park. Just a few minutes up the trail and you are at the **Powerlines Trail** that runs from Skyline to the Grouse parking lot. **MacKay Creek** runs adjacent to the park.

How To Get There

You can access this trail from Malaspina Place.

Hero's Rating: 🐾 🐾   **Human's Rating:** ★ ★

Mountain View Park

Park Number	n/a
Trail Difficulty	1 - 2
Trail Condition	Good
Time	15 minutes

This park is a bit of bush between the houses and the **Baden-Powell Trail**. There are a couple of ponds (I think the signs call the area Twin Lakes) which are exceptionally muddy.

How To Get There

You can access this trail from McNair Drive in Lynn Valley, just where it turns into Hoskins.

Hero's Rating: 🐾 🐾   **Human's Rating:** ★ ★

Seycove Park

Park Number	n/a
Trail Difficulty	unknown
Trail Condition	unknown
Time	unknown

This place was hard to find and the new maps aren't out yet, but according to the Parks Board this area is very small and situated between the school/community centre and Strathcona Road. There is supposed to be a trail in here but I couldn't find it.

How To Get There

You can access this trail from Strathcona.

Hero's Rating: No Paws   **Human's Rating: No Stars**

St. Albans Park

Park Number	n/a
Trail Difficulty	2 - 3
Trail Condition	Poor
Time	30 minutes

At the top of St. Albans there is an old access road that ends after about one block. The forest above this is riddled with trails which have been modified by armies of mountain bikers. Sounds worse than it is. The trails run across surprisingly level ground for the area, eventually linking with the **Braemar to Prospect Powerlines.**

How To Get There
You can access this trail at the top of St. Albans, off Braemar Road, at the top of Lonsdale.

Hero's Rating: 🐾 🐾   **Human's Rating:** ★ ★

Powerlines Trails

Park Number	70
Trail Difficulty	3 - 4
Trail Condition	Good to rustic
Time	2 - 4 hours

Almost anywhere there are powerlines you will find trails or roads beneath them. And, of course, the powerlines are kept clear of growth to a certain height. Here's a few of the better sections in North Vancouver. See **Princess Park** for the section that goes from there to 29th.

Braemar to Prospect

Park Number	70
Trail Difficulty	3 - 4
Trail Condition	Good to rustic
Time	2 hours

This trail follows the powerlines up the side of Grouse Mountain. It starts with a bit of a climb, but levels off after only a few minutes to roll across the ridge. This can be great on a nice day as it's out in the sunshine and has a good view of the city. Connects with **Baden-Powell** and **Old Grouse** trails at the top of Prospect Road. This is the top of **Mosquito Creek** trail as well. Lots of berries to be picked here.

You can then follow the **Baden-Powell Trail** to connect with the next bit of Powerline Trail.

How To Get There

From the Trans-Canada Highway (#1), take the Lonsdale exit (#18) and go north. Turn right on Braemar. Follow this road until you see the powerlines crossing overhead. The trail described climbs to the east.

Hero's Rating: 🐾 🐾   **Human's Rating:** ★ ★ ★

Skyline to Grouse Mt. Gondola Parking Lot

Park Number	70	
Trail Difficulty	3	
Trail Condition	Good	
Time	2 hours	

As with the **Braemar to Prospect** section this trail has open spaces and an occasional view. Unlike the other section it has no steep climb to begin with. The views of Vancouver city and the island across the water can be quite beautiful from this walk.

You can return on the **Baden-Powell Trail**, which you can access in the east corner of the parking lot.

How To Get There

From downtown Vancouver take Georgia Street to the Lions Gate Bridge. Take the North Vancouver off-ramp (right). Turn left on Capilano Road, the first intersection after the bridge.

From the Trans-Canada Highway (#1) in either direction take exit #14 (Capilano Road).

Follow Capilano Road north to Montroyal. Turn right (east) on Montroyal. Skyline goes north (up) from here. Follow Skyline to the top.

Or follow Capilano Road north to its end. The powerlines are plain to see on the east side of the parking lot.

Hero's Rating: 🐾 🐾   **Human's Rating:** ★ ★ ★ ★

Princess Park

Park Number	71	
Trail Difficulty	1 - 3	
Trail Condition	Good to rustic	
Time	30 minutes	

The entire park is not an Off-Leash Area so watch the signage. The park is riddled with trails through a dense evergreen forest which has been mostly cleared of underbrush. There is a nice creek and a field to run on. To the north of the park are powerlines with a very steep rustic trail. This leads down to 29th

Street and is an Off-Leash Area. If you follow the east side of the creek down a deer trail you can connect with **Hunter Park**.

How To Get There

Take the Trans-Canada Highway (#1) to Lonsdale, (exit #18). Take Lonsdale north to Osborne. Turn right on Osborne, which curves to the left when it meets Princess. There is a parking lot there.

Hero's Rating: 🐾 🐾 🐾   **Human's Rating:** ★ ★ ★

Rice Lake Road Trail

Park Number	72
Trail Difficulty	2 - 3
Trail Condition	Rustic
Time	1 hour

This trail is essentially a deer trail at this point but people are actively working on improving it as I write. It provides some excellent creek access to some very nice pools on the Seymour.

Although this is not officially part of the **Baden-Powell Trail**, people will start using it to connect these adjacent parts of the Baden-Powell, now that this trail is being improved. If you walk up Lynn Valley Road just a few paces from where it crosses Dempsey, you can veer right down Rice Lake Road. Just before this road goes onto private property, a trailhead opens up to the right (look for a fire hydrant and a couple of big rocks) and follows the creek to the parking lots at **Lynn Headwaters Regional Park**. The trailhead for the next step of the Baden-Powell is between the parking lot nearest to the Headwaters Park and the next nearest.

How To Get There

From the Trans-Canada Highway (#1) in either direction take exit #19 (Lynn Valley Road) and follow Lynn Valley Road northeast to where it seems to turn left onto Dempsey. Park somewhere along here, as parking is restricted down Rice Lake Road, which veers off to the right just on the other side of the intersection. Walk down the road, it's Off-Leash right away, past the footbridge that crosses the Seymour, to the trailhead.

Hero's Rating: 🐾 🐾 🐾 🐾   **Human's Rating:** ★ ★ ★ ★

Seymour Demonstration Forest

Park Number	73
Trail Difficulty	1 - 4
Trail Condition	Excellent to rustic
Time	1 - 5 hours

Fishing	Biking	Phone
Jogging	Water	Prohibited

Roads ▬▬ Trails ▪▪▪▪ Railways ┼┼┼┼ Road Block ┣━┫ Bridge ═══ Parking Lot (P) Off-Leash Area ▣ Water ▣ Parkland ▣

A large forested park situated in between **Lynn Canyon Park** and **Seymour Provincial Park**. The upper part of this park is off-limits to dogs, from the Rice Lake Parking Lot north, but there is a road which leads from the east of the Rice Lake parking lot and takes you down to the river and across at Twin Bridges (only one of which remains). The trail then heads down the east bank of the river to Riverside Drive. Along the way you can access the **Baden-Powell Trail** and other trails that climb **Mount Seymour,** like the Bridle Trail, Mystery Creek Trail, and others. All of these trails climb steeply through beautiful forests and you can link them together to create a number of different loop trails. Recent additions have improved signage in this park especially along the **Baden-Powell Trail**.

WARNING: The Seymour River current can be very strong. See **About Rivers** in the Trail Wisdom section of the book.

This is one of the best ways to access the trails in the foothills of Mount Seymour (see **North Shore Trails**). One of the drawbacks of this trail is the dirt road (**Lillooet Road**) leading in. Be aware that you will have to wash your car when you get home.

How To Get There

From the Trans-Canada Highway (#1) take exit #22. If you have been traveling eastbound turn left to the overpass across the highway.

Proceed straight through the lights, up the hill, past Capilano College and the graveyard. Lillooet Road continues as the dirt road that goes from the graveyard to the Rice Lake parking lot.

You can access this park from the west side of the Seymour, over a footbridge that crosses at Rice Lake Road, by Lynn Valley Road and Dempsey.

You can also access this park from Mount Seymour and from Riverside Drive. Be aware, however, that Riverside Drive is zoned for Resident Parking Only, May through September.

Hero's Rating: 🐾 🐾 🐾   **Human's Rating:** ★ ★ ★

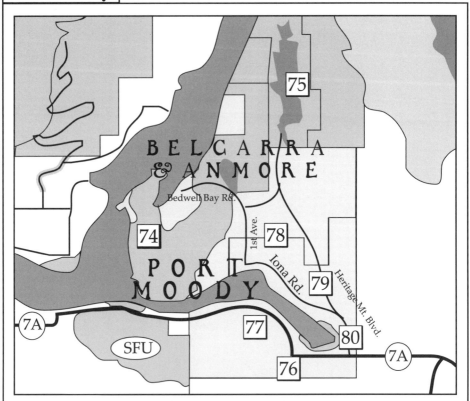

On the boardwalk on the Shoreline Trail.

Port Moody

(Including the Villages of Belcarra and Anmore)

Port Moody sits on the edge of the wilderness that surrounds Buntzen Lake. It also envelopes the end of Burrard Inlet, the tip of which is almost completely parkland.

Belcarra Regional Park

Park Number	74
Trail Difficulty	1 - 4
Trail Condition	Good
Time	6 hours

Swimming | Drinking | Phone
Fishing | Washroom | Water | Prohibited

Roads ▬ Trails ▪▪▪▪ Railways ┿┿┿┿ Road Block ⊢⊣ Bridge ⟋ Parking Lot Ⓟ Off-Leash Area ▪ Water ▪ Parkland ▪

Belcarra Regional Park is situated on the east shore of Indian Arm and is almost surrounded by water. There are several nice hikes and beaches. There are washrooms, a phone, and drinking water at the parking and picnic area.

Water quality in Indian Arm is Fair.

How To Get There

From the Barnet Highway (#7A) just east of Port Moody, turn left onto Ioco Road. Ioco takes a sharp left almost immediately. From here you can follow the signs to the park. On the way in you can visit a charming little old general store, the Pleasant Side Grocery. There is a right-hand turn on 1st Avenue, just before you would otherwise run into the oil refinery if you kept going.

Watch for "Park Full" advisories by the side to the road. In the summer this park is extremely popular with the locals.

Dogs are prohibited from parts of Sasamat Lake; White Pine Beach, on the swimming and fishing docks of the floating walkway, and at most pocket beaches along Sasamat Lake's shore. Don't go there. Proceed to the parking lot at the Belcarra Picnic Area.

Bedwell Bay Trail

Park Number	74
Trail Difficulty	1
Trail Condition	Good
Time	30 minutes

An easy stroll to a tidal mud flat. At Bedwell Bay you can sit and dream about how nice it must be to live in one of the fabulous houses that line the farther shore.

Hero's Rating: 🐾 🐾   **Human's Rating:** ★ ★

Jug Island Trail

Park Number	74
Trail Difficulty	3 - 4
Trail Condition	Good
Time	2 hours

This trail climbs up and down, sometimes steeply, through forests of broadleaf maple and hemlock to a small beach that faces northeast, toward Jug Island, just offshore, and up the Indian Arm. In summer you can swim here, but watch the tides. Add to the trail's time factor the amount of time you might want to sit on the beach and stare at the water.

Hero's Rating: 🐾 🐾 🐾   **Human's Rating:** ★ ★ ★ ★

Admiralty Point Trail

Park Number	74
Trail Difficulty	2
Trail Condition	Good
Time	1 hour

This trail hugs the water and passes by several small beaches and rocks. Add to the trail's time factor the amount of time you might want to sit on the beach and stare at the water. The view is not as nice on this side of the park; it looks back to the Barnet Highway and the sulphur piles.

Hero's Rating: 🐾 🐾 🐾   **Human's Rating:** ★ ★

Buntzen Lake Reservoir

Park Number	75
Trail Difficulty	1 - 5
Trail Condition	Good to rustic
Time	Endless

Fishing | Swimming | Drinking | Phone

Horses | Access | Washroom | Water | Prohibited

Dog Beach

Boat Drop Off

Dog Beach → Beach and Picnic Area

NO DOGS ALLOWED

Energy Nature Trail

Warden's Office

Dog Area

Bunsten Lake Trail

Buntsen Lake Trail

Powerhouse Rd.

Roads ▬ Trails ▪▪▪▪ Railways ┼┼┼┼ Road Block ⊢⊣ Bridge ⎓ Parking Lot Ⓟ Off-Leash Area ▣ Water ▪ Parkland ▪

A large wilderness park next to **Belcarra Regional Park**, Buntzen Lake positively crawls with people during the hot sunny weather. Often you can't even get your car into the park as they close off the access road when the albeit ample parking lots get full. There are trails to either side of the gate. Note that they are shared by horses.

I've included only Buntzen Lake Trail, but there are many other, slightly more rugged trails in this park as well, some with great views of Indian Arm. Pamphlets are available at the park or from BC Hydro (see appendices).

Although the trails are unsuitable for most handicapped folk, I have included this rating due to the easy access to the beach for you and your dog.

How To Get There

From the Barnet Highway (#7A) just east of Port Moody, turn left onto Ioco Road. You can follow the signs up the new route to Buntzen Lake; up Heritage Mountain Boulevard, right on Parkside, left on Aspenwood, right on East Road and right on Sunnyside. Or take the old Ioco Road (to the left) the same way you get into Belcarra Park (right on 1st), then take the Buntzen Lake turnoff from this road (right on Sunnyside).

Beach and Picnic Access

BC Hydro has kindly provided a couple places for you to take your dog when the main beach here is closed to them (May 15th through Oct. 1st). There are a couple of small sections of beach front on the extreme right- and left-hand sides of the main beach. Like the main beach, however, these doggie beaches are becoming overcrowded. There is also another area for dogs, with picnic tables(!), above the parking lots.

Buntzen Lake Trail

Park Number	75
Trail Difficulty	1 - 3
Trail Condition	Good
Time	4 - 5 hours

This trail leaves from the vicinity of the eastern dog beach if you are traveling counterclockwise around the lake. The trail is broad and fairly easy, dipping down to the lake now and again. The shore is generally lined with people fishing so take care your dog doesn't disturb them. At the far end of the lake is a small beach and picnic area. Across a narrows of crystal clear water is a suspension bridge. Afterward. there is a bit of a climb, but then the trail ambles back down to the water, and another bridge brings you back on a trail to the east end of the parking lot.

Hero's Rating: 🐾 🐾 🐾 🐾   **Human's Rating:** ★ ★ ★ ★

Chineside Park

Park Number	76
Trail Difficulty	2 - 4
Trail Condition	Rustic
Time	30 minutes

A steep ravine park tucked in between housing, this park straddles either side of Gatenbury Road, which plunges from Coquitlam down the hill into Port Moody. A very dense mixed forest with mossy maples and a couple of small creeks. A bit of a climb on a few very basic deer trails.

Late breaking news! There is a plan to designate a portion of this park as an Off-Leash Area on a one-year trial basis. Watch for new signage.

How To Get There
The small trails of this park can be accessed all around it. One main access to the east side of this park is the south end of Moody, just off St. John Street (the part of the #7 that runs through Port Moody). There are trailheads to the western side behind Kyle Park, and at Henry and Elgin.

Hero's Rating: 🐾 🐾　　　　**Human's Rating: ★ ★**

Easthill Park

Park Number	77
Trail Difficulty	1 - 3
Trail Condition	Good
Time	15 minutes

An urban park surrounded by housing, Easthill is aptly named, for it is built in terraces on the hillside. At the very top a path runs west above the line of houses. About a 15-minute round trip. The access point at Prince and Union takes you into fields and playgrounds at the bottom of the terraces.

How To Get There
From the Barnet Highway traveling southeast, turn right onto Gore Street which becomes Prince Street.

Hero's Rating: 🐾　　　　**Human's Rating: ★**

Flavelle Park

Park Number	78
Trail Difficulty	2 - 3
Trail Condition	Rustic
Time	Various

There are many trails that leave from the back of a kiddie playground and go off through the forest into the mountain area. Unfortunately, at this time there are no maps of this area, so be very careful if you venture in.

How To Get There

From the Barnet Highway (#7A) just east of Port Moody, turn left onto Ioco Road. Access off Flavelle Drive off Ioco Road.

Hero's Rating: 🐾 🐾   **Human's Rating:** ★ ★

North Shore Escarpment

Park Number	79
Trail Difficulty	2 - 3
Trail Condition	Rustic
Time	2 hours

The Escarpment is a forested area of land sandwiched between the houses below and the condo developments above. It has a nice forest, segmented by deep creek beds, through which run several trails, most of them deer trails and unreliable. From the east end of the park there is a fairly well developed trail that goes from Campbell Road and travels just under the line of condos, with good solid bridges built above the creeks. This trail currently ends at a new development, but perhaps one day soon it will continue around. Another trail starts at the west end of the park just above the school on Axford Bay.

How To Get There

From the Barnet Highway (#7A) just east of Port Moody, turn left onto Ioco Road. You can find a trailhead at the end of most of the roads on which you can make a right-hand turn from Ioco Road, starting with Campbell Road, and ending with Barber, which turns into Axford Bay by the schoolyard.

Hero's Rating: 🐾 🐾   **Human's Rating:** ★ ★ ★

Shoreline Trail
Including Rocky Point Park, Inlet Park, Old Mill Park, and Old Orchard Park

Park Number	80
Trail Difficulty	1 - 2
Trail Condition	Good
Time	2 hours

Fishing | Biking | Drinking | Phone | Off-Leash

Jogging | Access | Washroom | Water | Prohibited

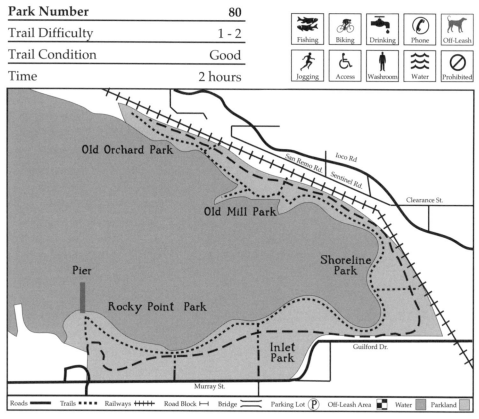

Roads ▬ | Trails ▪▪▪▪ | Railways ┼┼┼┼ | Road Block ┣━┫ | Bridge ═══ | Parking Lot (P) | Off-Leash Area ▣ | Water ▮ | Parkland ▯

The Shoreline Trail lines the tip of the arm of Burrard Inlet that Port Moody surrounds. Parts of the trail have raised walkways over tidal flats, that can be a lot of fun. Watch that your dog does not disturb the shorebirds, especially when they are nesting.

Rocky Point Park is a busy playground and picnic site with a pier for pedestrians. Old Mill Park has the ruins that stand out in the water of, you guessed it, an old mill, and the Old Orchard has a playground where your dog is not allowed.

The scenery across the water can be a bit industrial, what with the sulphur yard on one side and rows of condos on the other, but a very nice place just the same.

Water quality in Port Moody Arm is Fair.

Late breaking news! There is an Off-Leash Area being planned for a fenced-off portion of Rocky Point Park on a one-year trial basis. Look for new signage.

How To Get There
The Shoreline Trail may be accessed at, among other places, Rocky Point Park, 2800 block Murray Street, Inlet Park, 3200 block Murray Street, Old Orchard Park, 600 block Bentley Road, or from behind the recreation centre and city hall.

Hero's Rating: 🐾 🐾   **Human's Rating:** ★ ★ ★

Richmond

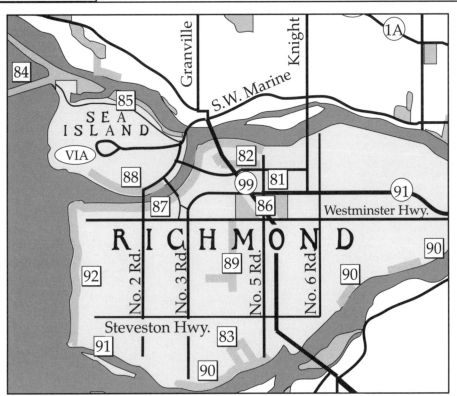

84
85
SEA ISLAND
VIA
88
87
92
No. 2 Rd.
No. 3 Rd.
R I C H M O N D
89
No. 5 Rd.
No. 6 Rd.
Steveston Hwy.
83
91
90
Granville
S.W. Marine
Knight
1A
82
99
81
86
91
Westminster Hwy.
90
90

Happiness is a wet dog–McDonald Beach Park

Richmond

Richmond has a couple of actual parks with trees and all, but the main attraction here is miles and miles of dyke walks. Just great on a sunny day.

Bath Slough

Park Number	81
Trail Difficulty	1
Trail Condition	Excellent
Time	15 minutes

A walk by a slough wedged tightly between warehouses and condos. An OK walk for a local, but the slough looks dirty and oily and the scenery isn't great.

How To Get There
Access off #5 Road north of Cambie, not off Cambie. Can also be accessed at various points in the neighbourhood.

Hero's Rating: No Paws   **Human's Rating: No Stars**

CN Trail

Park Number	82
Trail Difficulty	1
Trail Condition	Excellent
Time	1 hour

A nice little local trail that cuts straight as an arrow through a Richmond suburb. Lined with blackberry bushes. Watch out for intersecting roads.

How To Get There
Access east end of trail on Shell Road north of Bridgeport.

Hero's Rating: 🐾   **Human's Rating:** ★

Horseshoe Slough

Park Number	83
Trail Difficulty	1
Trail Condition	Fair
Time	15 minutes

Access

Water

A very minor walk through sparse trees that looks more promising on the map and at the trailhead than it turns out. The slough is mucky and muddy and the path runs between that and parking lots.

How To Get There
Access off Dyke Road.

Hero's Rating: No Paws   **Human's Rating: No Stars**

Iona Beach Regional Park

Park Number	84
Trail Difficulty	1
Trail Condition	Excellent
Time	30 minutes - 1 hour

Biking   Drinking   Phone

Access   Washroom   Water   Prohibited

Pacific Spirit Regional Park

North Arm Jetty

North Arm Fraser River

Vancouver

Georgia Straight

Iona Sewage Treatment Plant

Canfor Point Recreation Area

Sea Island Conservation Area

Iona Jetty

Ferguson Rd.

Sea Island Richmond

Roads ▬▬ Trails ▪▪▪▪ Railways ╫╫╫ Road Block ⊢⊣ Bridge ⚌ Parking Lot ℗ Off-Leash Area ◼ Water ▮ Parkland ▮

A park by the sea on the northwest tip of Sea Island. Dogs are not permitted in the marsh areas to the right of the parking lot as you enter. But even from the parking lot you can see all kinds of birds.

You can walk out on two jetties. The first, just before the parking lot, is very well groomed, like a seawall, to the point of being almost featureless. The second jetty, on the far side of the parking lot, is covered in logs and lined by beaches. There is a restricted lumberyard on this jetty, and lots of junk like rusting heavy machinery.

The sewage treatment plant right next door can make Iona Park an odiferous experience if the wind is coming off the land.

Water quality in the Fraser River North Arm is Fair.

How To Get There
Take Oak Street Bridge or Highway #99 to Sea Island Way, then take Sea Island Way west over the bridge toward the airport. Stay to your right all the way around the corner (watch for signage to Iona Beach and MacDonald Beach Parks), this will take you to Airport Road which becomes Grauer Road, which becomes Ferguson Road. Bear left at the sewage treatment plant.

Hero's Rating: 🐾 🐾   **Human's Rating:** ★ ★

McDonald Beach Park and Boat Launch

Park Number	85
Trail Difficulty	1
Trail Condition	Excellent to rustic
Time	30 minutes - 2 hours

Swimming	Biking	Drinking	Phone
Jogging	Access	Washroom	Water

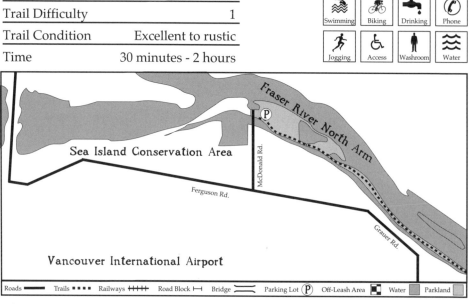

This park on the north side of Sea Island borders the North Arm of the Fraser River. There are many small trails through swampy grassland. Careful that your dog does not disturb the birds here, especially in nesting season. There is also quite a nice beach you can walk along, where you can watch the tugs go by. The dyke road mentioned in How To Get There runs east of the park. Another dyke runs west of the park, but this goes into the Sea Island Conservation Area, to which access is restricted. Currently there is no signage keeping you out, but it is apparently on the way.

Water quality in the Fraser River North Arm is Fair.

How To Get There

Take Oak Street Bridge or Highway #99 to Sea Island Way, then take Sea Island Way west over the bridge toward the airport. Stay to the right all the way around the corner (watch for signage to Iona Beach and MacDonald Beach Parks), this is Airport Road which will take you to Grauer Road.

You can access a dyke road (you and your dog, not your car) almost right away. Look for the dyke appearing on your right. It will take you to the park. Or you can continue along Grauer Road, turn right at McDonald Road, and park in the parking lot at the main part of the park.

Hero's Rating: 🐾 🐾 🐾   **Human's Rating: ★ ★ ★**

Richmond Nature Park

Park Number	86
Trail Difficulty	n/a
Trail Condition	n/a
Time	n/a

Dogs are not allowed at the Richmond Nature Park. However, just across Highway #99 there is another plot of land just as big as the Nature Park that is simply a **Nature Reserve**. There you can walk your dog and this is outlined.

Richmond Nature Reserve

Park Number	86
Trail Difficulty	1
Trail Condition	Rustic
Time	20 minutes

One of the few treed parks in Richmond. The park has one circular trail, very rustic, that winds through a very pretty forest of birch and pine. The ground is often boggy and wet, and there are a few pools and ponds dotted about. There is a covered picnic area.

How To Get There

Take Jacombs Road from north to south, park just before it terminates at the Westminster Highway, or access Jacombs off the Westminster Highway just west of Knight Street, near the Richmond Auto Mall.

Hero's Rating: 🐾 🐾   **Human's Rating: ★ ★**

Middle Arm Trail

Park Number	87
Trail Difficulty	1
Trail Condition	Excellent
Time	Various

An extensive dyke walk, the Middle Arm Trail starts at Terra Nova, the northwest corner of Richmond that overlooks the airport, and heads east along the Middle Arm of the Fraser River. The trail here is on-leash. It runs 3 km to the #2 Road bridge where some maps assure you there is a beach. Technically, I suppose, this is true. Just hope nobody gets there before you or there will be nowhere to sit down. The trail really peters out at the failed Bridgeport centre; a tall clock tower and the red roofs of the building mark the spot. Actually there is a nice pub here with a deck. Although I have biked past this point with some success, you have to cruise some back streets and cross some busy intersections. I don't recommend it with a dog. If you like, however, the trail does continue east, but it is much more fragmented than it looks on the map produced by the city of Richmond. There is another part between #4 Road and #5 Road, but this only affords about 15 minutes walking. I looked in vain for the trail that is supposed to run between #6 Road and the Knight Street Bridge.

Water quality in the Fraser River Middle Arm is Good.

How To Get There
Can be accessed at the north ends of #2, #3, #4, and #5 Roads, and generally along River Road to the east.

Hero's Rating: 🐾 🐾   **Human's Rating:** ★ ★

Sea Island Seawalk

Park Number	88
Trail Difficulty	1
Trail Condition	Excellent
Time	30 minutes - 1 hour

The seawalk north of the Dinsmore Bridge is ugly and dirty, and cars are allowed there. On the south side of the bridge, however, the trail is quite nice to walk, and continues under the #2 Road bridge to the seaplane terminal. Some interesting graffiti under this bridge, if you're into that.

Water quality in the Fraser River Middle Arm is Good.

How To Get There

Take either the #2 Road bridge or the Dinsmore Bridge over to Sea Island. Alternately, one could walk over the Dinsmore Bridge and turn right onto the trail.

Hero's Rating: 🐾 🐾 🐾   **Human's Rating:** ★ ★

Shell Road Trail

Park Number	89
Trail Difficulty	1
Trail Condition	Excellent
Time	1 hour

This path runs straight as an arrow (except for a little side arm to Francis Road) along the CN Railway tracks but separated from them by bushes, including some domestic blueberry gone wild, as well as some very nice silver or white birches. Hero proved me wrong when I assumed there was no water on this trail by finding, under a bush on the northernmost leg of the trail, one of the muckiest and yuckiest little sink-holes full of brown smelly water I have ever seen.

How To Get There

Access the north end of the trail where Shell Road ends at Westminster Highway. Access the south end of the trail where Shell Road ends a bit north of Williams.

A side access may be found at #4 Road and Francis.

Hero's Rating: 🐾   **Human's Rating:** ★

South Dyke Trails
Western Sections

Park Number	90
Trail Difficulty	1
Trail Condition	Excellent
Time	Various

The main track of South Dyke Trail runs beside the road, and is fine for walking your dog on-leash. One section is an Off-Leash Area and this goes from the south end of #3 Road and runs east as far as Finn Slough, more or less at the south end of #4 Road. If you've never seen Finn Slough, check it out. It has a small community of shacks on floats and stilts out in the slough itself; remnants of buildings built by the original Finnish population that was granted land (in a not very strict sense of the word) here.

Water quality in the Fraser River Main Arm is Fair.

How To Get There
Access at the south ends of #3 and #4 Roads.

Hero's Rating: 🐾 🐾   **Human's Rating:** ★ ★ ★

Eastern Sections

There are a few more sections further east, with the furthest east being by the new Fraserwood development right by Annacis Island. This bit is not bad, but it is right next to a smelly slough and is not as scenic as the more westerly arms of the walk.

There are also bits of dyke walk noted at the south end of #6 Road and one at the north end of Nelson. Don't bother.

Water quality in the Fraser River Main Arm is Fair.

How To Get There
From the east end of the Westminster Highway, take #9 Road or Fleetwood south to the water.

Hero's Rating: 🐾   **Human's Rating:** ★

Steveston Trail

Park Number	91
Trail Difficulty	1
Trail Condition	Excellent
Time	15 minutes

The Steveston Trail is quite developed and busy, running through downtown Steveston, and not really appropriate for dogs.

Hero's Rating: No paws   **Human's Rating:** ★

West Dyke Trail

Park Number	92
Trail Difficulty	1
Trail Condition	Excellent
Time	4 - 5 hours

The West Dyke Trail goes south from Terra Nova at the northwest tip of Richmond, all the way to Garry Point in Steveston, a walk of 5.5 km. It is very on-leash as it is very busy. On a weekend it can be as busy as Stanley Park's Seawall. The reason it's so busy, of course, is that it is quite beautiful, with blackbirds singing and marsh hawks gliding on the sea breeze.

Most of the amenities are in Steveston.

How To Get There

Access the north end of this trail at Terra Nova, the northwest corner of Richmond. Access the south end at Garry Point Park and Beach in Steveston. You can also access this walk at nearly any road that runs east to west; Steveston Highway, Williams, Francis, Blundell, and Westminster Highway.

Hero's Rating: 🐾   **Human's Rating:** ★ ★ ★

Surrey

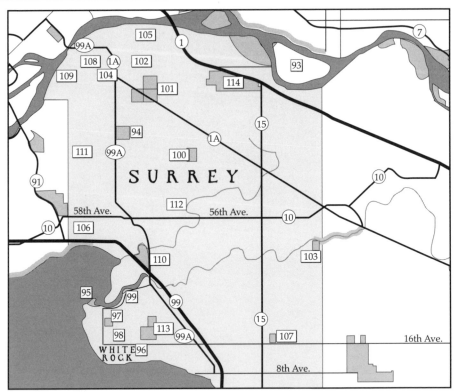

99A
105
1
7
108 1A 102
93
109
104
114
101
15
94
1A
111
99A
100
91
SURREY
10
58th Ave. 112 56th Ave. 10
10 106
110
103
95 99
99
97
98 113
107 16th Ave.
99A
WHITE 96
ROCK
8th Ave.

Blackie Spit near Crescent Beach.

Surrey
(Including White Rock)

Surrey is one of the booming areas of the GVRD and has many parks and green spaces to service their population, including a few Off-Leash Areas. In the south around White Rock and Crescent Beach there are beaches, most of which are closed to dogs during the warm weather.

Barnston Island

Park Number	93
Trail Difficulty	1
Trail Condition	Excellent
Time	3 hours

Barnston Island is circled by a paved road that some hiking books tout as a good place to go for a walk, and perhaps without a dog it could be. With a dog it is a complete pain; you have to keep dragging the dog off to the side as cars and farming vehicles squeeze by. The locals let their dogs run wild, so you are constantly having to police potential dogfights. The far side of the island, once you get to it, is not too bad, but here there are cows and horses that you mustn't let your dog annoy.

Barnston is a farming community, and thus is unlikely to enjoy hordes of people coming over on nice days in the summer, and while I will admit that the scenery is pretty, it is not any more so than many other walks in this area.

There is a Regional Park on Barnston Island, part of Surrey Bend Regional Park, but it consists of a tiny point with three picnic tables. Very nice for a picnic, to be sure.

Water quality in the Fraser River here is Good.

How To Get There

East of the Port Mann Bridge, turn off the Trans-Canada Highway (#1) at either 160th (exit 50) or 176th (exit 53) and head north. Take a right on 140th Avenue and this will take you to the free ferry. You can take your car onto the island, but you have to back off and on the ferry at the Barnston Island end.

Hero's Rating: 🐾   **Human's Rating:** ★

Bear Creek Park

Park Number	94
Trail Difficulty	1
Trail Condition	Excellent
Time	30 minutes

A busy urban park with sports fields, a formal garden, and a miniature train. Not a good place to flaunt the leash laws. There are well-kept trails (in fact some of them are paved) virtually all around this park, but the best area for dog walking is in the southeast corner of the park, where there is a creek. A bit too urban for me. Also the forest is young and not terribly exciting.

How To Get There

Access at corner of 88th Avenue and King George Highway. Another parking lot is on 140th, just south of 88th.

Hero's Rating: 🐾   **Human's Rating:** ★

Blackie Spit (Crescent Beach)

Park Number	95
Trail Difficulty	1
Trail Condition	Good
Time	30 minutes

The actual beach at Crescent Beach is closed to dogs between May 15 through September 15, but there is a part of Blackie Spit on which they may be walked. This is a level trail through grasslands that circles around by a canal, across which is an exceptionally pleasant looking community garden. You can get down to the water, but the shore is very mucky indeed.

In the winter you can walk the shore or the boardwalk.

Water quality in Boundary Bay is Fair.

How To Get There

Take Highway #99 south, then take exit #10 and keep bearing right, taking the road to Crescent Beach. You will cross a small one-way bridge, then turn right onto Crescent Road. Follow this into Crescent Beach. Turn right on Sullivan then right on Ohara.

Hero's Rating: 🐾 🐾   **Human's Rating:** ★ ★ ★

Centennial Park

Park Number	96
Trail Difficulty	2 - 3
Trail Condition	Good
Time	15 minutes

A few trails head into the woods down the bank behind the ice rinks. One of the trails goes out of the park and down the ravine to the ocean, but the condition of this trail is only fair.

How To Get There
Access off North Bluff Road (16th Avenue). Be prepared to pay for parking in this area.

Hero's Rating: 🐾   **Human's Rating:** ★

Crescent Beach
See **Blackie Spit**.

Crescent Park

Park Number	97
Trail Difficulty	1
Trail Condition	Excellent to good
Time	1 hour

Trails wind through a nice old forest. There is a series of lawns, that are very pretty, and a pond. Horse trails are clearly marked. The park also contains a sports field.

How To Get There
From Highway #99, take the White Rock exit (#10) and then head toward Crescent Beach. This will get you onto Crescent Road, which will turn into 128th Street Sunnyside Avenue (24th Avenue).

Hero's Rating: 🐾 🐾 🐾   **Human's Rating:** ★ ★ ★

Dogwood Park

Park Number	98
Trail Difficulty	1
Trail Condition	Good
Time	15 - 30 minutes

Some very wide trails riddle a small forest. A bit on the dull side, but it's an Off-Leash Area and there is a small pond for wading.

There is an equestrian paddock here so be careful with your dog around the horses.

How To Get There

Access off 20th Avenue between 128th and 140th Street.

Hero's Rating: 🐾 🐾   **Human's Rating:** ★

Elgin Park

Park Number	99
Trail Difficulty	1
Trail Condition	Good
Time	15 minutes

Based at historic Stewart Farm, now a weaving centre, and a marina, this park has a few small trails. One runs along the road southeast of the entrance at the farm, and one leaves the parking lot to the northwest and passes through a small wood, then circles a marshy area by the water.

Water quality in Boundary Bay is Fair.

How To Get There

From Highway #99, take the White Rock exit (#10) and then head toward Crescent Beach. This will get you onto Crescent Road. Follow just past 140th Street and look for the signs.

Hero's Rating: 🐾 🐾   **Human's Rating:** ★ ★

Fleetwood Park

Park Number	100
Trail Difficulty	1 - 2
Trail Condition	Good to rustic
Time	30 minutes

Fleetwood has a playground at its northern end, and a water park. The forest is fairly old with some evergreen mixed in with the deciduous.

The perimeter trail is very well groomed, but the inner trails are much more rustic and very muddy. A small creek runs through it. I saw a red-tailed hawk there.

How To Get There

Access on 80th Avenue at 160th Street. If you park by the big sports field, the trails leave from here.

Hero's Rating: 🐾 🐾   **Human's Rating:** ★ ★

Green Timbers Park

Park Number	101
Trail Difficulty	1
Trail Condition	Excellent
Time	1 hour

Surrounded by all kinds of development, Green Timbers has a nice evergreen forest through which trails have been cut, and a recent artificial lake with grassy areas around it. This area looks like a nice place to bring the kids on a hot day, (two moms and a half dozen blond kiddies were offloading as we left) although I'm sure the bottom of the new lake is muddy.

The main part of the park is bounded by 100th to 96th Avenue, and 140th to 148th Street. There is another section to the south, from 96th to 92nd Avenue, which is a bit less developed. There is one huge swath cut through from 140th to 148th Street that links to a biking trail along powerlines, as well as some deer trails.

How To Get There

The main park, the part with the lake, is accessed off 100th Avenue between 140th to 148th Street, where there is a parking lot. There are numerous trailheads around the park, notably on 148th. The northwest corner of the park, an educational centre, is off-limits to dogs.

Hero's Rating: 🐾 🐾   **Human's Rating:** ★ ★

Hawthorne Park

Park Number	102
Trail Difficulty	1
Trail Condition	Excellent
Time	15 minutes

Hawthorne has a playground at the entrance on 144th Street. This park only has a few small, very well groomed trails.

How To Get There
Access off 144th Street north of 104th Avenue.

Hero's Rating: 🐾   **Human's Rating:** ★

High Knoll Park

Park Number	103
Trail Difficulty	1 - 3
Trail Condition	Good to poor
Time	30 minutes - 1 hour

This park has two distinct sections, north and south of Colebrook Road. The south section has a forest of young evergreen trees honeycombed with trails. This area butts up against powerlines, with more trails.

The northern side of the park contains a meadow, that the Nicomekl River runs through, and which is quite muddy. This side of the park joins with the **Nicomekl River Park** and the Brydon Nature Reserve in Langley. There is a walkway that runs under powerlines on the north side.

Water quality in the Nicomekl River is Fair.

How To Get There
Access off Colebrook Road just east of 192nd Street.

Hero's Rating: 🐾 🐾 🐾   **Human's Rating:** ★ ★

Holland Park

Park Number	104
Trail Difficulty	1
Trail Condition	Excellent
Time	15 minutes

Just a few, mostly paved trails through a tiny forest surrounding grass fields.

How To Get There

Access off Old Yale Road and King George Highway.

Hero's Rating: 🐾　　　　**Human's Rating:** ★

Invergarry Park

Park Number	105
Trail Difficulty	2 - 4
Trail Condition	Fair to rustic
Time	30 minutes - 1 hour

A linear creek park, surrounded by development. There are a couple of old roads running through it, and it is not terribly pretty.

An old road starts off running south and at a gentle incline upwards along the side of the creek. This road branches to the right and becomes a trail that branches again as it goes south up the right side of the creek. The left branch that originally leaves the road goes up the left side of the creek. All the trails eventually have to climb out of the ravine, which has very steep sides. There are also rustic trails on a little plateau on the east side of the park and to the south.

How To Get There

Access off 166A Street. Take 108th Avenue right by the King George Highway, to Grosvenor, which splits off to the northeast. Go left on McBride, right on King, right on 116A Street.

From 108th Avenue take 148th Street which bears left as Wallace, then right as Surrey Street, then turn left on 116A.

Hero's Rating: 🐾 🐾　　　　**Human's Rating:** ★

Joe Brown Park

Park Number	**106**
Trail Difficulty	1 - 2
Trail Condition	Good
Time	30 minutes

A small forest with a few minor trails, a quarry/landfill dump, and a tiny mucky stream. Really not a lot to commend this park, unless you want to use the paddock for your horses.

How To Get There

From the intersection of the King George Highway (#99A) and Highway #10, take 56th Avenue, turn left on 128th, right on 56th Avenue, right on 125A Street.

Hero's Rating: No Paws   **Human's Rating: No Stars**

Redwood Park

Park Number	**107**
Trail Difficulty	1 - 3
Trail Condition	Good to fair
Time	30 minutes

You don't have to go to northern California to see redwoods. The Brown twins lived in this area in the late 1800s and they planted a number of exotic tree species, including some redwoods, that have now matured into a fine stand. Also there is a treehouse here that commemorates one that the brothers actually lived in. There are some long, covered picnic tables and a sloping lawn, below which is a wilder deciduous forest and a short level walk on an old railway.

How To Get There

There is a driveway and parking lot that you can access at the north edge of the park, off 20th Avenue. The park goes down a steep hill to 16th Avenue, but there is only a small pullout by the side of the road.

Hero's Rating: 🐾 🐾   **Human's Rating:** ★ ★ ★

Royal Kwatlin Park

Park Number	108
Trail Difficulty	1
Trail Condition	Good
Time	10 minutes

A few trails run through a small forest in the northwest corner.

How To Get There

Access off Old Yale Road just north of 104th Avenue.

Hero's Rating: 🐾   **Human's Rating:** ★

Scott Hill Park

Park Number	109
Trail Difficulty	2 - 3
Trail Condition	Rustic
Time	10 minutes

Basically a bit of bush around a ravine.

How To Get There

Access off River Road just west of 120th Street.

Hero's Rating: 🐾   **Human's Rating:** ★

Serpentine Fen Bird Sanctuary and Nature Trails

Park Number	110
Trail Difficulty	1
Trail Condition	Excellent
Time	30 minutes

This park is a nature reserve, and as such is a bad place to flaunt the leash laws. The park consists of marshes and grassland surrounded by farmland and the odor of manure is sometimes quite powerful. Be careful that your dog does not disturb the waterfowl, especially in nesting season.

There are level dyke walks on both sides of the Serpentine. The dykes are very tall here and have steep packed-earth walls. The one on the north is the longer of the two. Both end up at the highway, and while you can get under the bridge, it's a scramble and you could easily end up trapped on the other side by the tide. Also the dykes between the highway and the water are not quite as nice as some others (see **Boundary Bay Regional Park**) and Hero managed to cut his paws somewhere along the way. There is No Trespassing signage on the eastern side of the Serpentine dyke below the highway, but also above the highway, which is confusing, as this is one of the main paths in the Fen. It is also possible to cross the highway's bridge (no fishing or loitering, says the sign) to get from one side of the Serpentine to the other, but exercise extreme caution.

There is another trail that leaves from the southern dyke and enters the marsh. This runs near the highway for a while and ends up in a second parking lot.

Water quality in the Serpentine River is Fair.

Water quality in Boundary Bay is Fair.

How To Get There
Access off the west side of the King George Highway (#99A), just north of Highway #99. There is a parking lot here just south of the Serpentine River.

Hero's Rating: 🐾 🐾   **Human's Rating:** ★ ★ ★

Strawberry Hill Powerlines

Park Number	111
Trail Difficulty	1
Trail Condition	Good
Time	10 minutes

An open-air walk under powerlines. This is a very decent attempt to turn powerlines into parkland. There are a few gravel trails and a couple of ponds have been made.

How To Get There
Access to the south of 80th Avenue between 124th and 128th.

Hero's Rating: 🐾   **Human's Rating:** ★

Sullivan Park

Park Number	112
Trail Difficulty	1
Trail Condition	Excellent
Time	15 minutes

Behind a complex of sports fields there are a few meadows interconnected by a small trail system. Lesser deer trails go into a small woods.

How To Get There
Access from 62A Avenue, off 152nd Street.

Hero's Rating: 🐾   **Human's Rating:** ★

Sunnyside Acres Urban Park

Park Number	113
Trail Difficulty	1 - 2
Trail Condition	Excellent to poor
Time	1 - 2 hours

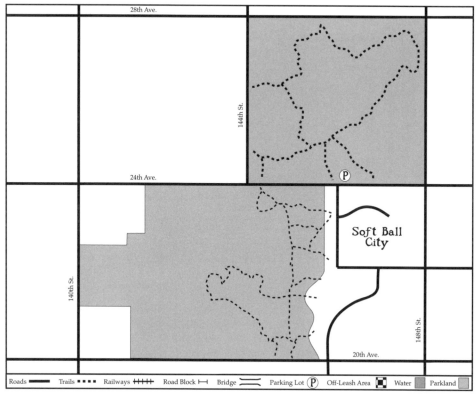

| Roads ▬▬ | Trails ▪ ▪ ▪ ▪ | Railways ┼┼┼┼ | Road Block ├─┤ | Bridge ⟋ | Parking Lot Ⓟ | Off-Leash Area ◼ | Water | Parkland |

Trails run through a forest of medium density.

The northern half of the park is the more developed and has the nicest forest; one of those fabulous treed vistas that features seemingly endless, evenly spaced tree trunks fading off into the distance. Trails are well maintained in this area, and one trail is even "Obstacle Free."

The southern half (below 24th Avenue) has some good trails on its east side, but the western side is riddled with deer trails that twist and turn and flood in the wet season. Beware of getting lost and turned around down in this part of the park.

How To Get There

You can get into this park from any street that adjoins it, but there is a parking lot on 24th Avenue just east of 144th Street.

Hero's Rating: 🐾 🐾   **Human's Rating:** ★ ★ ★

Tynehead Regional Park

Park Number	114
Trail Difficulty	1 - 2
Trail Condition	Excellent
Time	5 hours

♿ Access   Off-Leash

Washroom   Water   Prohibited

Roads —   Trails ■■■■   Railways ┼┼┼┼   Road Block ⊢⊣   Bridge ⤳   Parking Lot (P)   Off-Leash Area   Water   Parkland

Tynehead is a lightly forested and well-established park centered around a small stream.

Water quality in the Serpentine River is Fair.

How To Get There

Take Trans-Canada Highway (#1) to 160th Street exit (#50–6.5 km east of the Port Mann Bridge) and follow the signs to the park; left on 103rd Avenue, that curves around, left on 102nd Avenue to the 168th Street park entrance and parking lot. The Off-Leash Area is right there.

From the 176th Street exit (#53) go west on Tynehead Drive, which becomes 101st Avenue; turn north on 168th, then left into the parking lot. There is another parking lot on 161st Street.

Off-Leash Area

Park Number	114
Trail Difficulty	1 - 2
Trail Condition	Excellent
Time	30 minutes

Off-Leash

The Off-Leash Area contains a path that winds through small fields of tall grasses divided from one another by copses of trees. Hero enjoyed bounding through the tall grass. The park would be a good place to train a dog in tracking.

Hero's Rating: 🐾 🐾 🐾   **Human's Rating:** ★ ★ ★

Serpentine Loop Trail

Park Number	114
Trail Difficulty	1 - 2
Trail Condition	Excellent
Time	1.5 hours

The established trails in the rest of the park circle the Serpentine River through a mixed forest with many vine maples and broadleaf maples. Very pretty in the fall. There are many signs asking people (Not just dogs!) to keep out of the stream. (Fish live here!) Having to keep out of the water lowered Hero's Rating below.

Hero's Rating: 🐾 🐾 🐾   **Human's Rating:** ★ ★ ★

Vancouver

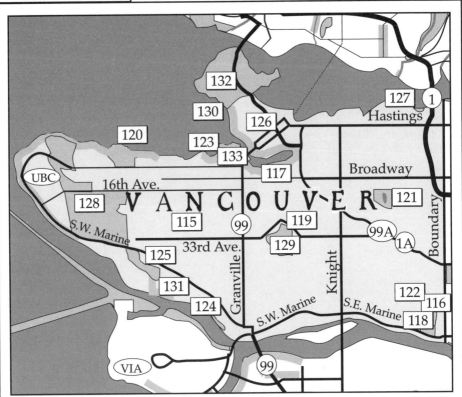

132
130
126
120
123
133
117
127 1
Hastings
Broadway
UBC
16th Ave.
V A N C O U V E R
121
128
S.W. Marine
115
99
119
99A
1A
Boundary
125
33rd Ave.
129
Knight
131
Granville
124
S.W. Marine
S.E. Marine
122
116
118
VIA
99

Looking across to Wreck Beach

Vancouver

With the greatest population density in the GVRD, Vancouver has the toughest problems with parks, especially where dogs are concerned. In recent years this battle has heated up with the Off-Leash issue coming to a head and the formation of the Vancouver Dog Owners Association.

For an area that houses our downtown, Vancouver has a number of quite large parks. Chief among these for most folks is Stanley Park, with its Seawall that will eventually extend all the way around False Creek and all the way to Pacific Spirit Park out by the University, which is Off-Leash and probably the best park in Vancouver for dog walking.

Balaclava Park

Park Number	115
Trail Difficulty	1
Trail Condition	Excellent
Time	15 minutes

This is basically a playing field. One of four parks designated in a pilot project as an Off-Leash Area from 6:00 am to 10:00 am and after 5:00 pm to midnight. Don't go here if you're not a local, as it's not worth traveling to, and you'll mess up the test.

Hero gives this one paw, but only because of the Off-Leash Area.

How To Get There

Access this park off Caernarvon or Balaclava between 31st and 29th. Thirty-third is the nearest main artery.

Hero's Rating: 🐾   **Human's Rating: No Stars**

Captain Cook Park

Park Number	116
Trail Difficulty	1
Trail Condition	Good to rustic
Time	15 minutes

Nice little local park. A couple of broad swaths cut through with gravel trails, as well as a number of rustic trails through the woods.

How To Get There
Access off Champlain and 54th.

Hero's Rating: 🐾   **Human's Rating:** ★

Charleson Park

Park Number	117
Trail Difficulty	1
Trail Condition	Excellent to good
Time	30 minutes

Charleson Park, although quite small, is a very nice downtown park. There are treed areas with paths, grass fields, as well as a pond (that you should probably keep your dog out of, as it's usually full of waterfowl). There is access to water (ocean) on a sloped part of the seawall. Sometime in the near future this park will be included in the **Seawall**, as it will circumnavigate False Creek.

Water quality in False Creek is Borderline.

How To Get There
Access off Charleson Street, which runs just north of 6th Avenue between Granville Island and the Cambie Bridge.

Hero's Rating: 🐾 🐾 🐾   **Human's Rating:** ★ ★ ★ ★

Everett Crowley Park

Park Number	118
Trail Difficulty	1 - 2
Trail Condition	Good to rustic
Time	30 minutes - 1 hour

Here's a real sleeper. This one's not even on the map as a park yet and it only recently acquired a sign. It looks like just a vacant lot–most of it is overgrown with blackberry, but there are several wide, well-maintained trails that circle around the park, as well as a number of deer trails, through a young forest of alder. There are also a couple of nice little ponds in the northeast corner.

How To Get There
Access this park off Kerr just north of SE Marine Drive.

Hero's Rating: 🐾 🐾 🐾   **Human's Rating:** ★ ★ ★

Hillcrest Park

Park Number	119
Trail Difficulty	1
Trail Condition	Excellent
Time	5 minutes

This is basically a playing field. One of four parks designated in a pilot project as an Off-Leash Area from 6:00 am to 10:00 am and after 5:00 pm to midnight. Don't go here if you're not a local, as it's not worth traveling to, and you'll mess up the test.

Hero gives this one paw, but only because of the Off-Leash Area.

How To Get There

Access this park from the part of 33rd that jags around Queen Elizabeth Park. Turn north on Dinmont just west of Nat Bailey Stadium.

Hero's Rating: 🐾   **Human's Rating: No Stars**

Jericho Beach Park

Park Number	120
Trail Difficulty	1
Trail Condition	Excellent to good
Time	1 hour

In addition to the beach, which your dog is only welcome on from to November 1st to May 30th, there are a number of trails that circle a pond, and a few near 4th Avenue, in the south and southwest of the park, that wind between some trees.

Jericho Beach has large complicated signs about dogs and their place in society. Good place to get a ticket for not complying with leash laws.

Jericho connects to a long seaside walk that goes west around Point Grey, passing Locarno Beach and Spanish Banks, after which it enters **Pacific Spirit Regional Park** .

Water quality in English Bay is Fair.

How To Get There

Access from the west end of Point Grey Road or from 4th Avenue west of Alma.

Hero's Rating: 🐾 🐾   **Human's Rating: ★ ★**

John Hendry Park (Trout Lake)

Park Number	121
Trail Difficulty	1
Trail Condition	Excellent
Time	15 minutes

Good-sized open grassy park with a small lake. Lots of activity here.

How To Get There
Around Nanaimo, Grandview Highway splits into North and South Grandview, the latter of which turns into 12th right by the park. There is a parking lot near where Victoria becomes Commercial.

Hero's Rating: 🐾   **Human's Rating:** ★

Killarney Park

Park Number	122
Trail Difficulty	1
Trail Condition	Good
Time	5 minutes

This is basically a playing field. One of four parks designated in a pilot project as an Off-Leash Area from 6:00 am to 10:00 am and after 5:00 pm to midnight. Don't go here if you're not a local, as it's not worth traveling to, and you'll mess up the test.

Hero gives this one paw, but only because of the Off-Leash Area.

How To Get There
Access off Kerr and 49th.

Hero's Rating: 🐾   **Human's Rating: No Stars**

Kits Beach Park

Park Number	123
Trail Difficulty	1
Trail Condition	Excellent
Time	10 minutes

A really busy beach in the summer, Kits beach can be a great place to greet or take leave of the day. Unfortunately but understandably, dogs are not allowed on the beach itself. You can walk them on the **Seawall** and on the lawn (provided they aren't the usual places dogs aren't allowed; picnic areas, playgrounds, etc.). Expect to meet lots of other dogs here.

Water quality in English Bay is Fair.

How To Get There

Kits Beach is on Cornwall just over the Burrard Street Bridge from downtown.

Hero's Rating: 🐾   **Human's Rating:** ★

Marine Drive Foreshore Park

Park Number	124
Trail Difficulty	1
Trail Condition	Excellent to good
Time	30 minutes

This park is a little marshy strip along the north bank of the Fraser, just across from **McDonald Beach** on Sea Island in Richmond. There are boardwalks in several places as well as a pier. There are some nice sandy beaches where a dog can go in the water without getting too muddy.

Water quality in the Fraser River North Arm is Fair.

How To Get There

From SW Marine Drive just east of Granville, turn south on Angus. There are a few parking spots.

Hero's Rating: 🐾 🐾   **Human's Rating:** ★ ★ ★

Musqueam Park

Park Number	125
Trail Difficulty	1
Trail Condition	Fair to rustic
Time	30 minutes

There is a manicured part of the park which faces SW Marine, but behind this and over Crown Street are rustic trails running through a small forest. Be aware that the Musqueam Band has a reserve here and be careful not to trespass. Connects with a nice walk down to the water at **Southlands**.

How To Get There

From SW Marine Drive, turn south on Crown, Highbury, Olympic, Wallace, or Holland.

Hero's Rating: 🐾 🐾   **Human's Rating:** ★ ★

Nelson Park

Park Number	126
Trail Difficulty	1
Trail Condition	Excellent
Time	5 minutes

This is basically a playing field. One of four parks designated in a pilot project as an Off-Leash Area from 6:00 am to 10:00 am and after 5:00 pm to midnight. Don't go here if you're not a local, as it's not worth traveling to, and you'll mess up the test.

Hero gives this one paw, but only because of the Off-Leash Area.

How To Get There
Located at Nelson and Thurlow in downtown Vancouver.

Hero's Rating: 🐾   **Human's Rating: No Stars**

New Brighton Park

Park Number	127
Trail Difficulty	1
Trail Condition	Good
Time	15 minutes

New Brighton Park is a small grassy field on the shore of Burrard Inlet, right beside the PNE and the wheat pool. There is also an outdoor swimming pool.

Good beach access for a dog, as the beachfront is small and (I assume) not very attractive for sunbathers.

Water quality in Burrard Inlet here is Fair.

How To Get There
New Brighton can be accessed from the off-ramp approaching McGill Street or from Bridgeway Street. The entrance to the park is a sharp right into the parking lot, which one can only hope will survive with the new roadwork presently being done here. You can drive down to the park itself, but parking is almost nonexistent. There are some empty lots the truckers use down on Bridgeway that seem to be OK for parking.

From Hastings take the approach to the Second Narrows Bridge, then turn left at the light before you get to the bridge. This will take you past Gate 9 of the PNE. A right turn at the 3-way stop will get you onto Bridgeway. From Burnaby you can take N. Skeena through a tunnel under the approach to the Second Narrows Bridge. This will take you to Bridgeway Street. From the Second Narrows Bridge traveling south, take the far right exit toward McGill Street.

Hero's Rating: 🐾 🐾   **Human's Rating:** ★ ★

Pacific Spirit Regional Park

Park Number	128
Trail Difficulty	1
Trail Condition	Excellent to fair
Time	15 minutes - 6 hours

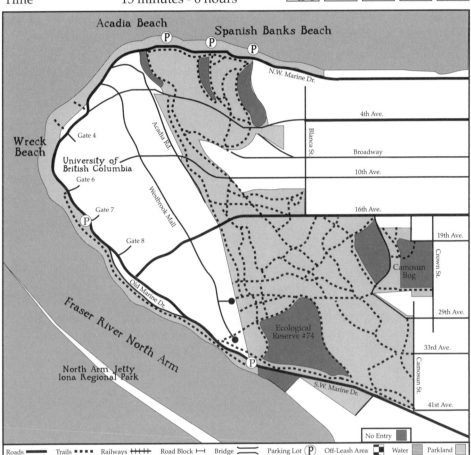

A large, mainly forested park but one that is patched together between roads and university buildings. To date this is the only place in the city of Vancouver where you can walk your dog Off-Leash at any time of day. There are over 35 km of trails in the 763 hectares of this park. Some are multipurpose (riding, cycling, walking) and a few are just for hiking. The trails comprise a web through forests of fir and huge old broadleaf maples and delicate vine maples. Lots of little creeks and ponds and mudholes here. Quite busy with cyclists.

The park includes Ecological Reserve #74, Camosun Bog, and other ecologically sensitive areas not open to the public. The GVRD's pamphlet on the area gives a write-up on Camosun Bog under a heading of special features, but if there is anything to see, we didn't find it. The bog seems to be fairly inaccessible.

Please note that your dog is not allowed on the beaches between April 1st and October 30th.

Water quality in English Bay is Fair.

How To Get There
Follow 4th Avenue west until it becomes Chancellor Boulevard. There are places to park along Chancellor Boulevard, above the beach trailheads, but parking is at a premium all around the university, both when classes are in session as well as on sunny weekends.

Or, follow SW Marine Drive west. There is a historical monument with a small parking lot on the south side of the road. You can park up and down the road here as well, and there is a trailhead just across the boulevard from the monument.

Or, follow 16th Street west to the park centre 400 metres west of Blanca Street. There is no parking here however.

Hero's Rating: 🐾 🐾 🐾 🐾   **Human's Rating:** ★ ★ ★ ★

South Portion

Park Number	128
Trail Difficulty	1 - 3
Trail Condition	Good to fair
Time	30 minutes

There is an area just above Acadia Beach and Spanish Banks Beach that is separate from the main area of the park. Here you can escape the busier part of the park, though the trails here are a bit steeper, following creek beds up from Marine Drive to Chancellor Boulevard.

How To Get There
Take NW Marine Drive to Spanish Banks or Acadia Beach.

Hero's Rating: 🐾 🐾 🐾 🐾   **Human's Rating:** ★ ★ ★ ★

The Beaches

Park Number	128
Trail Difficulty	2 - 4
Trail Condition	Good to poor
Time	15 minutes - 6 hours

Pacific Spirit Park also includes the beaches around Point Grey and the Fraser Foreshore. Please note, however, that your dog is not allowed on the beach between April 1st and October 30th. This prohibition extends to the mucky foreshore of the Fraser, probably for ecological reasons, as it's nowhere you'd want to sunbathe. There are many trails that lead from Marine Drive down to the shore. Or, if you want to walk along the shore, you can begin as far east as **Jericho Beach**, walk past Locarno and Spanish Banks, and eventually enter the park at Acadia Beach where clothing on the beach becomes optional. Not many nudists between November 1st to May 30th, however. There is a bit of a path here, but eventually you have to walk on the beach itself. The beaches continue with Tower Beach and Wreck Beach, Point Grey and Point No Point. You will know you've come to the end of the beaches when you reach a sandy point with a stone jetty (the North Arm Breakwater) where the beach folk have erected logs as flagpoles and to hang hammocks on. Some of these have interesting carvings on them.

By the time you leave Wreck Beach you are on the foreshore of the Fraser and the beaches are tiny, few, and far between. The shore is mucky, and overgrown with cattails, which the waterfowl love. The path becomes a muddy scramble along the bank over fallen logs. This continues until you run into the Musqueam Indian Reserve. The last trail up the bank climbs back to the Historical Landmark parking lot.

Water quality in English Bay is Fair.

How To Get There
There is a free parking lot at Acadia Beach, the last before the university, where parking is a nightmare, and another on the far end of the beaches, east of the university on SW Marine Drive. You can also park on Old Marine Drive, where there are many trailheads leading down, or just east of this at the Historical Landmark parking lot.

Hero's Rating: 🐾 🐾 🐾 🐾   **Human's Rating:** ★ ★ ★ ★

Queen Elizabeth Park

Park Number	129
Trail Difficulty	1 - 2
Trail Condition	Excellent
Time	30 minutes

Not a really great place for dog walking, but a very nice open field park dotted with trees and a lovely formal garden. The grounds include some grassy hills with the occasional tree.

How To Get There
Access off 33rd between Cambie and Main.

Hero's Rating: 🐾   **Human's Rating:** ★ ★

Seawall

Park Number	130
Trail Difficulty	1
Trail Condition	Excellent
Time	Many hours

To walk the entire Vancouver Seawall would take many, many hours. I've never done it and I'm not going to hazard a guess at how long it would take. **Stanley Park** alone takes several hours to get around, and the Seawall stretches from the Georgia Street entrance of Stanley Park, circles the park, then carries on past First Beach and into False Creek. (Some day soon it will entirely encircle False Creek). For now you have the option of crossing Granville Street Bridge and then carrying on to the west (though you'd miss Granville Island and **Charleson Park** if you did). It passes through **Vanier Park** and **Kits Beach**, after which it kinda peters out along Point Grey Road and picks up again at **Jericho Beach** where it joins with several beaches and, eventually, **Pacific Spirit Park**.

The Seawall gets incredibly busy on nice days, especially weekends and throughout tourist season.

Water quality in English Bay and Vancouver Harbour is Fair.

Water quality in False Creek is Borderline.

How To Get There
Go to the park of your choice. Start there.

Hero's Rating: 🐾   **Human's Rating:** ★ ★

Southlands

Park Number	131
Trail Difficulty	1
Trail Condition	Good to fair
Time	1 hour

Horses, horses, and more horses. Southlands is an semiurban area south of Kerrisdale where there are many riding stables and some grand homes that look like they belong in the country. Starting from **Musqueam Park**, you can walk down a trail that runs just east of the Musqueam Indian Reserve and, eventually, just west of the Point Grey Golf Course. A very muddy ditch runs along the edge of the reserve. The people at the Point Grey Golf Course have very nicely created a path between their course and the water that you can then walk along. The path continues past Deering Island to the foot of Blenheim, where some industry takes over the shore. If you want to continue, a couple of blocks down Celtic Street you will arrive at the McCleery Golf Course which has also created a path on their foreshore that you may walk. Unfortunately, the walk does not continue under Marine Drive Golf Course, which comes next, and that's a real shame, for it is all that lies between this walk and the **Marine Drive Foreshore Park**.

Water quality in the Fraser River North Arm is Fair.

How To Get There

Go to **Musqueam Park**; from SW Marine Drive, turn south on Crown, Highbury, Olympic, Wallace, or Holland.

Or go down into Southlands at the south end of Blenheim. Note please, that the speed limit in Southlands is 30 kmh. Watch for horses on the road.

Hero's Rating: 🐾 🐾 🐾   **Human's Rating:** ★ ★

Stanley Park

Park Number	132
Trail Difficulty	1 - 2
Trail Condition	Excellent
Time	Various

Fishing	Swimming	Biking	Drinking	Phone
Horses	Jogging	Access	Washroom	Water	Prohibited

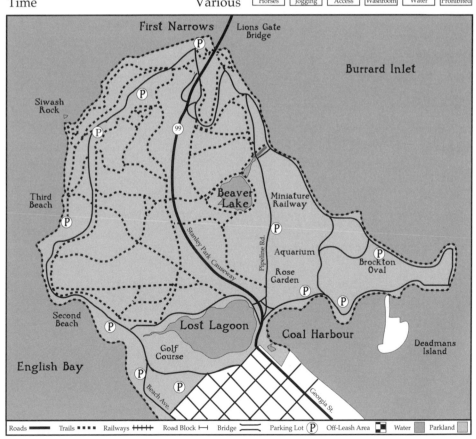

Roads ▬ Trails ▪▪▪▪ Railways ┼┼┼┼ Road Block ⊢⊣ Bridge ⚊ Parking Lot Ⓟ Off-Leash Area ◼ Water ▢ Parkland ▢

One of the world's truly great city parks, Stanley Park has some great trails for walking your dog, but you must keep your dog leashed and this is rather more strictly enforced than most other parks due to population densities. Dogs are prohibited from the beaches. Personally, I would stay away from the **Seawall** and the area around the aquarium and formal gardens. Head instead for the northern part of the park, roughly between Siwash Rock and Beaver Lake. Take care, however, around the cliffs.

Water quality in English Bay and Vancouver Harbour is Fair.

How To Get There
Stanley Park can be reached from downtown Vancouver via Georgia Street. It can be reached from the North Shore via the Lions Gate Bridge. Expect to pay for parking throughout the park.

Hero's Rating: 🐾 🐾   **Human's Rating:** ★ ★ ★ ★

Trout Lake
(See **John Hendry Park**)

Vanier Park

Park Number	133
Trail Difficulty	1
Trail Condition	Excellent
Time	5 Minutes

Vanier Park is the rolling lawn between the water and the planetarium. There is a pond with a statue in it. This park lies between Granville Island and **Kits Beach** on the seawall. Often there are people here flying kites.

Water quality in English Bay is Fair.

Water quality in False Creek is Borderline.

How To Get There
Go south over Burrard Street Bridge and take the first right. Follow this road past the planetarium to the water.

Hero's Rating: 🐾   **Human's Rating:** ★ ★

West Vancouver

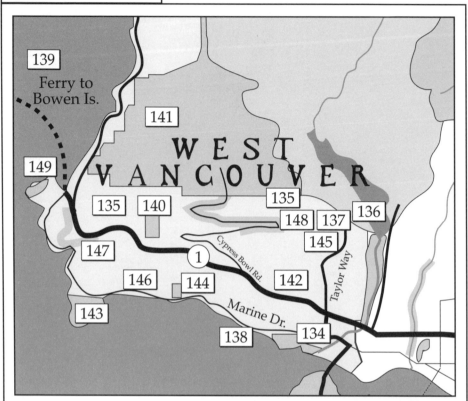

139
Ferry to
Bowen Is.

141

WEST
VANCOUVER

149

135 140

135

148 137 136

147

145

1

Cypress Bowl Rd.

142

Taylor Way

146 144

143

Marine Dr.

138 134

The view of Fisherman's Cove from the Seaview Walk is lost on some.

West Vancouver

West Vancouver has many parks, some by the seashore and others in the mountains, containing some of the GVRD's most breathtaking vistas. With North Vancouver District, West Van is leading the way with many areas designated for Off-Leash dog walking.

North Shore Mountain Trails

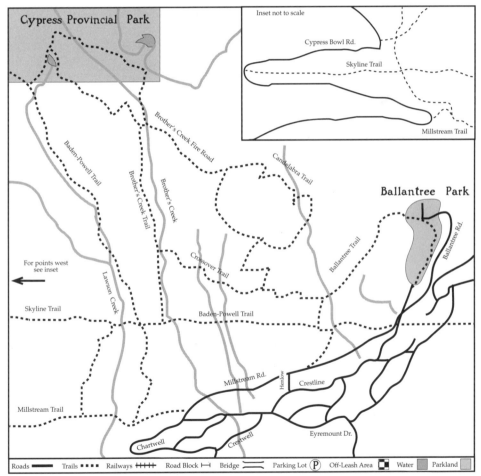

There are several trails on the North Shore that run across the south side of the mountains, through dense evergreen forests, above the line where houses have been built (thus far) in West Vancouver. Many of them cross through other parks such as **Cypress Provincial Park** and **Capilano River Regional Park**, and they all intertwine as they cross the mountains. All of these trails run through dense evergreen forests, some of which are first growth.

The **Brothers Creek Trail, Skyline Trail,** and **Ballantree Trail** crisscross and intersect with the **Baden-Powell** (For the eastern part of the **Baden-Powell** see under this heading in North Vancouver).

West Vancouver's pamphlet on dogs lists Cypress Ridge as an Off-Leash Area. Though there seems to be some confusion about exactly where this is, it would seem to include the area containing the aforementioned trails, above Millstream and below Cypress Provincial Park (which is not Off-Leash).

It is very easy to mix and match these trails, going up one trail and coming back down the other and still arriving at your car. It is also, apparently, quite easy to get lost. West Vancouver has excellent trail markings with guideposts at the main trail intersections, but there are many smaller "deer trails" which are being increasingly used by cyclists which in turn makes them more substantial trails. These trails are generally quite rustic and overgrown, and are poorly marked in some cases, and so can lead you astray if you are not careful. They will eventually take you back to one of the larger trails, but it might take some doing to get back to where you parked your car.

Ambleside Beach

Park Number	134
Trail Difficulty	1
Trail Condition	Excellent
Time	15 - 30 minutes

Open-air, ocean sidewalk. The Off-Leash Area is a lawn dotted with bush at the eastern part of the park and a beach just below the pitch and putt. Weekends and even weekdays can be crowded with many dogs, so be prepared for your pooch to do lots of schmoozing with other animals. Hero is a fairly social dog, but finds this place a bit overwhelming at times.

If you arrive by foot along the **Capilano Pacific Trail,** then you arrive at the Off-Leash Area when you enter the park just after going under the train tracks. If you come by car, stay to your left in the parking lot and look for a road that cuts behind the sport fields to the pitch and putt and the fitness track.

The West Vanners are very progressive and have doggie poop-bag dispensers, and even a doggie water bowl chained to a freshwater tap.

Water quality in English Bay is Fair.

How To Get There

You can access this park right at the beach off Marine Drive, just inside West Vancouver. Over the Lions Gate Bridge, take the West Vancouver turnoff and follow Marine Drive west, just past Park Royal shopping centre. You can walk to Ambleside from the Dam at the top of **Capilano River Regional Park.** You can also access this park at the south end of the Park Royal parking lot. A trail leads to the beach.

Hero's Rating: 🐾 🐾 🐾 🐾 🐾   **Human's Rating:** ★ ★ ★ ★

Baden-Powell Trail

Park Number	135
Trail Difficulty	1 - 4
Trail Condition	Rustic
Time	Many hours

Drinking	Phone	Off-Leash
Swimming	Washroom	Water

These are the parts of the Baden-Powell in West Vancouver. For points east on this trail see this heading under North Vancouver.

Glenmore to Millstream

Park Number	135
Trail Difficulty	2 - 4
Trail Condition	Rustic
Time	3 - 5 hours

Off-Leash

This trail goes along powerlines through the suburban British Properties, climbing very steeply, crossing several roads (keep your dog close) until it finally enters the forest just after crossing Millstream. The forest here can be dark and gloomy on a rainy day in a kind of Tolkienesque way that we mad West Coast, rain forest types really like; or it can be nice and cool on a hot day.

How To Get There

The easiest way to access this trail is by doing it in conjunction with the previous walk from the Cleveland Dam. However, you can also take the Trans-Canada Highway (#1) to the Taylor Way turnoff (exit #13) and go north on Taylor Way, taking the right-hand turn where it ends in just a couple of blocks. This is Stevens, which you follow until you reach Deepdene where you turn right. Shortly you will come to Glenmore, where you can turn left, but there's not much of a trailhead, so good luck.

Hero's Rating: 🐾   **Human's Rating:** ★ ★

Millstream to Cypress

Park Number	135
Trail Difficulty	3 - 4
Trail Condition	Rustic
Time	4 - 6 hours

Off-Leash

Heavily-wooded trail on the side of the mountain. From Millstream west the trail is the same trail as the **Skyline Trail** for quite a distance. The trail here is really lovely, with well-worn, old bridges and stairs going through a couple of ravines including **Brother's Creek**.

Eventually the Baden-Powell and Skyline Trails diverge, with the Baden-Powell climbing steeply. The trail climbs straight up the side of the mountain arriving near Blue Gentian Lake in **Cypress Provincial Park.** (Please note that the Off-Leash privilege does not continue into Cypress Park.) It then disperses into the many trails that circle the lakes there. You can walk up the road to get to the last leg of the trail, which is a long one.

How To Get There

You access this part of the trail from the very top of the British Properties. Take the Trans-Canada Highway (#1) to the Taylor Way turnoff (exit #13) and go north on Taylor Way. Whether you go right or left is of no matter, as there are myriad ways you can end up on Millstream, which is right at the top. Take, for instance, Southborough to Eyremount to Crestline to Henlow to Millstream. The main routes have stronger painted lines.

There are access points along Millstream Road just after it leaves from Chartwell Drive and further east just after Henlow.

Hero's Rating: 🐾 🐾 🐾   **Human's Rating:** ★ ★ ★ ★

Cypress to Eagleridge

Park Number	135
Trail Difficulty	3 - 4
Trail Condition	Rustic
Time	8 - 10 hours

A heavily-wooded trail on the side of the mountain. Please note that Cypress Park is not an Off-Leash Area, though the rest of the trail is. One of the longer parts of the trail, and the steepest, it starts at the top parking lot at **Cypress Provincial Park**, climbs steeply, then descends past a series of lakes, (look for the fire-bellied newt) and then dives down the mountain to Eagleridge. You may want to tackle this one starting at Eagleridge, and get the worst of the climb over with early. You may even want to cut this section of the trail in half, doing one part from Eagleridge up to the lakes and back, and the upper half from the Cypress parking lot up over the hill and then down to the lakes, and back.

How To Get There

Both Eagleridge (exit #2A) and Cypress Park (exit #8) can be accessed off the Trans-Canada Highway (#1).

Hero's Rating: 🐾 🐾   **Human's Rating:** ★ ★ ★

Ballantree Park

Park Number	136
Trail Difficulty	2
Trail Condition	Rustic
Time	1 hour

This park is a small forest on a rocky bluff with a few small clearings. Ballantree Trail, however, is a major trail that climbs into the mountain to meet the Baden-Powell and Brothers Creek Trails.

How To Get There

This park is at the very top of the British Properties. Take the Trans-Canada Highway (#1) to the Taylor Way turnoff (exit #13) and go north on Taylor Way. Whether you go right or left is of no matter, as there are myriad ways you can end up where you need to go. Take, for instance, Southborough to Eyremount to Crestline to Henlow to Millstream to Kildonan to Ballantree. The main routes have stronger painted lines.

Ballantree Park Trail

Park Number	136
Trail Difficulty	2 - 3
Trail Condition	Rustic
Time	30 minutes

One trail runs from Ballantree Road down to Kildonan Road. The District of West Vancouver's Dog Regulations literature lists this park as an Off-Leash Area (except playground and Fitness Circuit). The only evidence I could find of the former is a small overgrown clearing and the latter would seem to consist of a set of metal parallel bars and push-up bars situated on a side trail near the trailhead–there is no track such as you would want to run on. I don't think either gets much use.

Hero's Rating: 🐾   **Human's Rating:** ★

Ballantree Trail

Park Number	136
Trail Difficulty	3
Trail Condition	Rustic
Time	1 hour

Heavily-wooded trail on the side of the mountain. This trail goes up to the **Brother's Creek Fire Road**. This junction is marked by one of West Van's excellent trail markers, as well as by the ruins of the 1912 mill boiler house and base of a steam sawmill. Remains of a donkey engine exist in the woods nearby. What you will actually see is an old stone wall and some concrete foundations. If you are interested in this sort of thing, call the District of West Vancouver Parks and Recreation Department listed in the appendix of this book, and ask them for their *Shakes, Shinglebolts and Steampots* flyer that outlines a hike through these woods to visit several such sights. There is an extremely unofficial (as there is No Camping in this area) "camping" spot just below the trail where a side trail, marked with orange spray paint, goes down to the **Baden-Powell Trail**.

Hero's Rating: 🐾 🐾   **Human's Rating:** ★ ★ ★ ★

Brothers Creek Trail

Park Number	137
Trail Difficulty	4 - 5
Trail Condition	Fair to rustic
Time	4 - 5 hours

Heavily-wooded trail on the side of the mountain. **Brothers Creek Trail** climbs steadily up the mountain and ends in **Cypress Provincial Park,** around Blue Gentian Lake. Even in late spring we encountered snow here, which made finding the trail a real challenge. You can then take the **Baden-Powell Trail** back down if you wish.

How To Get There

This park is at the very top of the British Properties. Take the Trans-Canada Highway (#1) to the Taylor Way turnoff (exit #13) and go north on Taylor Way. Whether you go right or left is no matter, as there are myriad ways you can end up where you need to go. Try, for instance, Southborough to Eyremount to Crestline to Henlow to Millstream. The main routes have stronger painted lines.

Hero's Rating: 🐾 🐾 🐾   **Human's Rating:** ★ ★ ★ ★

Centennial Seawalk

Park Number	138
Trail Difficulty	1
Trail Condition	Excellent
Time	1 hour

An open-air walk on a paved seawall. From 19th to 24th Street you can let your dog run on the track side of the chain-link fence beside the seawall. Note that there is nothing between your dog and the train tracks, though it doesn't seem that there are any problems arising from this fact. Hero can't get to the water, and the path is pretty dull, but the view of the harbour is fabulous.

Water quality in English Bay is Fair.

How To Get There

Access at anywhere from Ambleside Park to Dunderave Park. Just head for the water.

Hero's Rating: 🐾   **Human's Rating:** ★ ★

Crippen Regional Park (Bowen Island)

Park Number	**139**
Trail Difficulty	1 - 3
Trail Condition	Excellent to rustic
Time	Many hours

Horses	Swimming	Biking	Phone
Jogging	Access	Washroom	Water	Prohibited

Roads ▬▬ **Trails** ▪▪▪▪ **Railways** ╫╫╫╫ **Road Block** ⊢⊣ **Bridge** ⪦ **Parking Lot** (P) **Off-Leash Area** ◪ **Water** ▨ **Parkland** ▢

A 15-minute ferry ride from Horseshoe Bay, Crippen Park started life as a resort in the 1920s. The park sports a good-sized lake, wonderful forests, and fabulous views of rocky seashores. A small trail runs between the Lagoon and the shore by a partly sandy / mostly rocky beach.

How To Get There

The Trans-Canada Highway (#1) ends at Horseshoe Bay (as far as the Mainland is concerned). From here you can take a ferry to Bowen Island. Crippen Park is so close to the terminal on Bowen that you can walk on and off the ferry. Parking in Horseshoe Bay is limited, however, and as taking a bus with a dog is not an option, you are reduced to driving on or finding parking in Horseshoe Bay.

Alder Grove Trail/Maple Trail

Park Number	139
Trail Difficulty	1 - 2
Trail Condition	Excellent
Time	30 minutes

These trails leave from behind the old Union Steamship Company Store on the main drag right off the ferry. They climb past the Memorial Garden and the Lagoon to Bridal Veil Falls where there is a fish ladder that must be great fun when the salmon are spawning.

Hero's Rating: 🐾 🐾 🐾   **Human's Rating:** ★ ★ ★

Killarney Creek, Hatchery, and Meadow Trails

Park Number	139
Trail Difficulty	1 - 2
Trail Condition	Good
Time	1 hour

There are a number of trails running between Bridal Veil Falls and Killarney Lake. Killarney Creek Trail, which goes all the way to the lake's picnic area, runs on the edge of a forest of fir and cedar, right next to the Terminal Creek Meadows, which is a large grassy area circled by very pretty stands of birch and maple. Where the Hatchery Trail and the Meadow Trail meet is an equestrian ring, so watch for horses here.

Hero's Rating: 🐾 🐾 🐾 🐾   **Human's Rating:** ★ ★ ★ ★

Killarney Lake Loop Trail

Park Number	139
Trail Difficulty	1 - 2
Trail Condition	Good
Time	2 hours

The trail that circles Killarney Lake walks you through some of the nicest forest anywhere on the planet. Great old cedars, Douglas fir and some of the gnarliest, old broadleaf maples I've ever seen. The ground cover is a riot of ferns, and moss covers everything. On the far side of the lake is a boardwalk with a solitary bench looking out onto the lake through a stand of dead trees (looks better than it sounds, actually).

Hero's Rating: 🐾 🐾 🐾 🐾   **Human's Rating:** ★ ★ ★ ★

Dorman Point Trail

Park Number	139
Trail Difficulty	3 - 4
Trail Condition	Good
Time	30 minutes

From the Snug Cove Picnic Area, a trail climbs up to a high rocky bluff that overlooks Howe Sound back toward Horseshoe Bay and out toward Point Grey. It's a bit of a climb, quite steep, but the view is truly inspiring.

Hero's Rating: 🐾 🐾   **Human's Rating:** ★ ★ ★ ★

Cypress Falls Park

Park Number	140
Trail Difficulty	2 - 4
Trail Condition	Rustic
Time	1 - 2 hours

A forested park surrounding a substantial creek, Cypress Falls Park is one of West Van's best kept secrets. The trails climb through old growth forest containing some impressive Douglas firs, and the creek, which has cut itself into a rocky crevasse, is sparkling clear and icy cold even on a sweltering August day. The falls are a little tough to get to, so unfortunately dunking yourself under them is not in the cards, but the view of them from the cliffs is worth the walk.

You start off on a trail that roughly follows the creek and should lead you to a little lookout just below the first bridge. Below this lookout is the first set of falls. If you continue up this trail you will pass by a series of deep pools carved out of the canyon rock, like a mini **Lynn Canyon**. These looked so inviting for a paddle, but the canyon was so much cooler than the surrounding forest that the only taker was Hero, who waded and swam with delight. Continue on this way to reach the upper falls.

Another way to go is to cross the first bridge and continue up this trail to the old fire road. You will walk by a power station and a municipal yard, then cross another bridge. Bearing to the right will take you on a fire road to **Cypress Provincial Park**. Turn to your left along the road and look for a trail heading back down toward the creek. This will lead you to the lookout for the upper falls. You can then follow the path back down the west side of the creek.

There are so many trails in this park, and they are completely unmarked at this point (rare for West Van) so it's hard to know where one begins and the other leaves off. Please be careful in this park–it would be easy for the neophyte woodsman to get lost.

How To Get There

From the Trans-Canada Highway (#1) take the Woodgreen exit (#4), turn right immediately; this will take you to Woodgreen Drive, where you will turn right. Turn left onto Woodpark Road. One of the trailheads is here.

Hero's Rating: 🐾 🐾 🐾 🐾   Human's Rating: ★ ★ ★ ★

Cypress Provincial Park

Park Number	141
Trail Difficulty	2 - 5
Trail Condition	Good to rustic
Time	Various

Biking | Drinking | Phone
Swimming | Washroom | Water | Prohibited

Roads ▬ Trails ■■■ Railways ┼┼┼┼ Road Block ┝┥ Bridge ⟗ Parking Lot Ⓟ Off-Leash Area ▨ Water ▩ Parkland ▨

An enormous wilderness park containing alpine areas and mountain forests. There are many great trails in Cypress, including parts of the **Baden-Powell Trail**, and they link up with trails that climb into the park from the British Properties. There are pamphlets available from the Province and maps at the top of the road, where the trails begin, to show you the way. Some great swimming can be had in the small lakes along the trails.

How To Get There
Take the Trans-Canada Highway (#1) to the Cypress Park turnoff (exit #8).

Hero's Rating: 🐾 🐾   **Human's Rating:** ★ ★ ★ ★

Douglas Woodward Park

Park Number	142
Trail Difficulty	3
Trail Condition	Rustic
Time	30 minutes

A forested park. For what appears on the map to be a rather insignificant park, Douglas Woodward has a veritable maze of trails, and two substantial creeks. There are many access points to this park. Nothing I'd make a trip across town for, but very nice for a local walk. The east-most trail actually goes down the creek all the way to the highway.

How To Get There
From the Trans-Canada Highway (#1) take the 21st Street exit (#10). Turn right on Westhill Drive. Follow this to Westhill Place or Westhill Drive.

Hero's Rating: 🐾 🐾   **Human's Rating:** ★

Lighthouse Park

Park Number	143
Trail Difficulty	1 - 3
Trail Condition	Good
Time	1 - 3 hours

One of our truly great parks, featuring broad trails through thick forests on the ocean side. A must-see whether you are a local or from out of town; it is an excellent park for those who want to get a feel for the old growth forest without venturing too far out into the wilderness. Lighthouse Park has some of the biggest, grandest old Douglas firs and cedars you will ever have the privilege of setting your eyes on. As an example of West Coast coastline it is unparalleled, with craggy, rocky bluffs lining the water, resplendent with firs, pines, and arbutus trees. The trails are a delight to walk and have the air of long use but without the tarnish that often accompanies it. They almost all circle back to the parking lot–either that or they run up against urban neighbourhoods.

At Point Atkinson there is a lighthouse and an old camp.

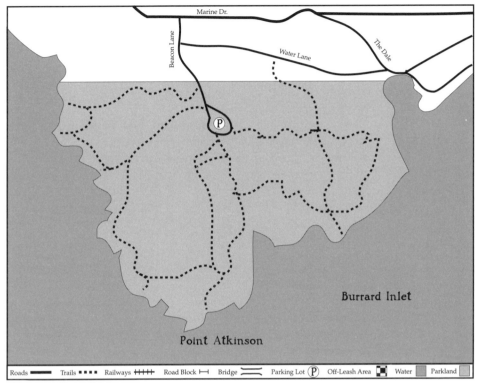

How To Get There

Take Marine Drive west to just past Keith Road, which comes down from the Caulfield area. Turn left at the park sign (carefully, as it is hard to see over the crest of the hill here).

Hero's Rating: 🐾 🐾 🐾 🐾   **Human's Rating:** ★ ★ ★ ★ ★

McKechnie Park

Park Number	144
Trail Difficulty	2 - 3
Trail Condition	Good to rustic
Time	30 minutes

This park is mainly forested, with a few clearings. The trails climb up to a high rock, just above a set of tennis courts, that has a rather cool turret built in stone with an unusual three-branched seat on top. Another strange artifact in this park is the carcass of an old tractor.

How To Get There

This park can be accessed from any of the streets that surround it. Sharon Street off Marine Drive is one way. Parking is very limited.

Hero's Rating: 🐾   **Human's Rating:** ★

Millstream Trail

Park Number	145
Trail Difficulty	1 - 4
Trail Condition	Good to fair
Time	2 - 3 hours

A heavily-wooded trail on the side of the mountain. One of the many trails above the British Properties, this trail is relatively flat as it runs across, not up, the mountainside, dipping into the creeks it passes. The trail terminates on Millstream Road on the east and at Cypress Bowl Road to the west.

How To Get There

This trail can be accessed at the first eastern hairpin turn on the road up to **Cypress Provincial Park**. Take the Trans-Canada Highway (#1) to Cypress Bowl Road (exit #8).

It can also be accessed from Millstream Road at the top of the British Properties. Take the Trans-Canada Highway (#1) to the Taylor Way turnoff (exit #13) and go north on Taylor Way. Whether you go right or left is no matter, as there are myriad ways you can end up on where you need to go. Try, for instance, Southborough to Eyremount to Crestline to Henlow to Millstream. The main routes have stronger painted lines.

Hero's Rating: 🐾 🐾 🐾   **Human's Rating:** ★ ★ ★ ★

Piccadilly Park

Park Number	146
Trail Difficulty	2
Trail Condition	Rustic
Time	5 minutes

A bit of bush with very minor trails. Suitable for local walking only. There are a couple of rocky outcroppings that can be accessed which look right out onto the train tracks. Must be exciting when a train goes by.

How To Get There

Take Marine Drive to Keith to Piccadilly North.

Hero's Rating: No Paws   **Human's Rating: No Stars**

Seaview Walk

Park Number	**147**
Trail Difficulty	1 - 3
Trail Condition	Excellent
Time	1.5 hours

An open-air walk along the side of the hill above Marine Drive. As its name promises, there are many lookouts on this trail where you can see the ocean. The views are great and the trail flat and wide. Just right for a nice easy stroll on a sunny day. In particular there are a number of great views of Fisherman's Cove, one of Vancouver's most scenic and exclusive marinas. At the east end of the trail is Nelson Creek, which is clear and cold with a rocky bed. Just here at the east end is the only part of the trail that is not level. Garbage containers appear at either end of the trail as well as one in the middle. There are even one of those dispensers of plastic bags at each end of the trail to encourage you to pick up after your pet.

How To Get There
Follow Marine Drive to the Gleneagles Golf Course. Park in the lot across the road, on the north side of Marine Drive. On the east end of the walk you can find Cranly Drive on the map and start from there.

Hero's Rating: 🐾 🐾 🐾   **Human's Rating:** ★ ★ ★ ★

Skyline Trail

Park Number	**148**
Trail Difficulty	4 - 5
Trail Condition	Fair to rustic
Time	4 - 5 hours

A heavily-wooded trail on the side of the mountain. Skyline Trail runs across the mountain and is much less of a climb than some of the trails above the British Properties. There are some great views to be had from here. The trail dips in and out of several creeks (careful on the old wooden bridges, some of them are in disrepair) and ends up on the powerlines just before terminating in the second parking lot/viewpoint on the road up to Cypress Park.

How To Get There
This trail is at the very top of the British Properties. Take the Trans-Canada Highway (#1) to the Taylor Way turnoff (exit #13) and go north on Taylor Way. Whether you go right or left is of no matter, as there are myriad ways you can end up on where you need to go. Try Southborough to Eyremount to Crestline to Henlow to Millstream. The main routes have stronger painted lines.

Hero's Rating: 🐾 🐾 🐾   **Human's Rating:** ★ ★ ★ ★

Whytecliff Park

Park Number	149
Trail Difficulty	2 - 3
Trail Condition	Rustic
Time	30 minutes

Whytecliff is a park with a well-known diving area and beach that your dog is not allowed anywhere near. Another part of the park has been set aside as Off-Leash, however. The trail climbs steeply at first, then levels out to wander around typical West Van moss-covered, rocky bluffs. Arbutus trees abound and you get little peek-a-boo views of the water. Lots of places to picnic on a nice day. The trails all loop around to come back to the parking lot.

How To Get There

Take Marine Drive to Horseshoe Bay. When you reach the 5-way stop, go through on the same street as the Fire Hall. Signs will lead you to the park. Don't go in the first parking lot. Dogs are not allowed in the west part of Whytecliff park, so if you want to use most of the amenities you will have to leave them in the car. Go to the "overflow" parking lot. The trail leaves from the east end of this lot.

Hero's Rating: 🐾   **Human's Rating:** ★ ★

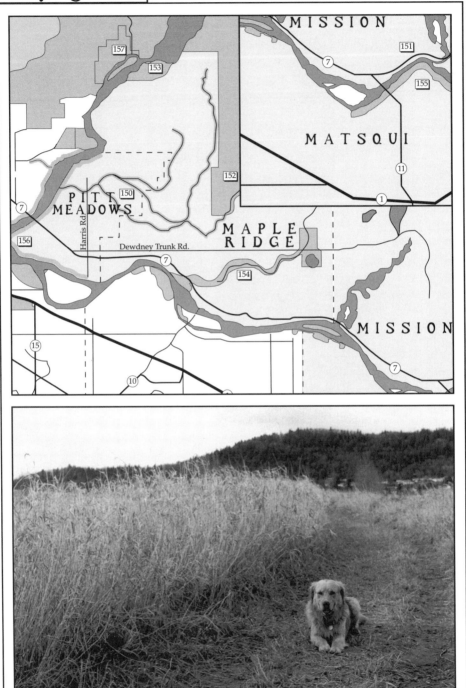

A brief pause on the Matsqui Trail.

Outlying Areas

(Including Maple Ridge, Pitt Meadows, Matsqui, and Mission)

Crossing the Pitt River or venturing out past Surrey, one finds acres and acres of farmland and wilderness. There are communities out there, to be sure, but still lots of room to move about.

Alouette River Dykes (Pitt Meadows)

Park Number	150
Trail Difficulty	1
Trail Condition	Excellent to good
Time	2 hours - unlimited

It don't get much better than this, folks. Beautiful countryside with mountains in the distance, a nice, fairly clean river, and miles and miles of flat, groomed dykes to walk. Fabulous place for biking. Nearly the entire length of the dykes is wheelchair accessible.

There are dykes on both sides of the Alouette and you can walk west from Harris to the **Pitt River**, where there are more dykes, or east into the farming country. Note that the Alouette splits into two arms pretty well right away, and you have to go as far as Neaves Road before you can cross. Even then, if you try and return on the other side of the river branch you are on, you will find yourself in the "V" shaped part of the "Y" and will have to walk through this to get to the other side and return to Harris; not undoable, but a long walk of four hours or more. Walk one side or the other, which will take about 2 hours to complete, or start at Neaves Road and walk the inside of the "V."

Note: the dyke on the north side of the river east of Neaves Road is closed between Oct. 1 and Dec. 31st. There are signs to this effect.

The etiquette for these dykes is that pets be leashed around other dyke users. In other words, don't let your unleashed dog run up to people, which of course you wouldn't do at any time, any where.

Water quality in the Alouette River is Fair.

How To Get There

Take the Lougheed Highway (#7) east of the Pitt River. Turn left on Harris. Follow Harris and park where it crosses the Alouette River.

Hero's Rating: 🐾 🐾 🐾 🐾 🐾   **Human's Rating:** ★ ★ ★ ★ ★

aser River Heritage Park (Mission)

Park Number	151
Trail Difficulty	1 - 3
Trail Condition	Good to rustic
Time	30 minutes - 1 hour

An open-field park with a few trails around the edges. From the carpark you will see a few fields and a couple of buildings. You can walk along the ridge for the view. There are a few groomed trails on the far side of the fields from the car park, and these will take you to more trails of a more rustic nature. There is a fairly clean creek.

How To Get There
From the Lougheed Highway (#7) just east of Mission, turn up Stave Lake Street, then go right on 5th.

Hero's Rating: 🐾 🐾   **Human's Rating:** ★ ★

Golden Ears Provincial Park (Maple Ridge)

Park Number	152
Trail Difficulty	Various
Trail Condition	Good to rustic
Time	1 hour and up

Because it's rather far away, I'm not going to go into too much detail about this park except to tell you that it's there, it's huge, and it's wild. Please be aware that this is a wilderness area and be prepared.

Your dog is prohibited access to the beach areas.

See the appendix in the back of the book for the phone number of the BC Parks Board. They have many informative pamphlets which they are glad to send you.

How To Get There
Take the Lougheed Highway (#7) to Haney. Get onto the Dewdney Trunk Road, either where it branches off the #7 at the border of Pitt Meadows and Maple Ridge, or by taking 216th Street north. Go east on the Dewdney Trunk. Turn north on 232nd Street. Follow this to where Fern Crescent connects at Maple Ridge Park. Follow Fern Crescent east into the park.

Hero's Rating: 🐾 🐾 🐾 🐾   **Human's Rating:** ★ ★ ★ ★

Grant Narrows Regional Park (Pitt Meadows)
including the Pitt-Addington Marsh Wildlife Management Area

Park Number	153
Trail Difficulty	1 - 2
Trail Condition	Excellent to poor
Time	1 - 4 hours

Fishing · Swimming · Biking · Phone
Jogging · Access · Washroom · Water

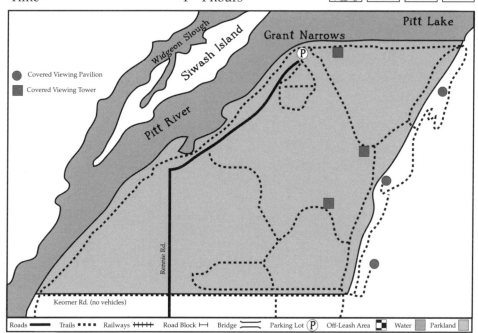

Mainly a park of dyke-walks through a large marsh on the edge of the Pitt River and Pitt Lake, with some trails up on the mountainside as well.

Grant Narrows Regional Park actually only encompasses the boat-launch area, but it is the gateway to the **Widgeon Marsh Reserve**, as well as the "Pitt Unit"–the Pitt Meadows side of the **Pitt-Addington Marsh Wildlife Refuge**. The other half, the **Addington Marsh**, is reached through **Minnekhada Regional Park** in Port Coquitlam. The park's boundaries are hard to discover, so the area on the map noted as the park is the actual marsh area and those trails to the right of this are on the mountainside.

The main dyke takes off out of the park and heads down the Pitt River (see **Pitt Meadows Dykes**) and is a good route for cyclists, who are not allowed in the rest of the marsh.

Dykes circle through the marsh with beaver lodges and waterfowl all around. Take care that your dog does not disturb the wildlife, especially during nesting season. The dykes either have a narrow grassy trail like the one around the Addington Marsh, or are broad and clear like a regular dyke. There are several raised viewing platforms on the dykes.

This park also has some trails on the wooded slopes of the mountain next to the marsh. They are quite steep, but they reach great little covered viewing pavilions built on the side of the hill with fantastic views.

Apparently this area has lots of bears, so beware o' the bear.

Water quality in the Pitt River is Good.

How To Get There
From the Lougheed Highway (#7), take Harris Road north and follow the GVRD signs. They are currently rerouting and changing roads there, so this is the best advice I can give you at this time. You can also access the dyke walks on Rannie Road and Keorner Road on the way in.

Hero's Rating: 🐾 🐾 🐾 🐾   **Human's Rating:** ★ ★ ★ ★

Kanaka Creek Regional Park (Maple Ridge)

This park is spread out and broken into several different parks, so this is how it is described. I have been canoeing up Kanaka Creek, before we got Hero, and you can put in at Fraser Riverfront Park. I'm really not sure how Hero would do in a canoe.

Water quality in Kanaka Creek is Fair.

Fraser Riverfront Park
Riverfront Trail

Park Number	154
Trail Difficulty	1
Trail Condition	Excellent
Time	1 hour

The trail leaves the parking lot and heads past an observation tower on the creek, down to the banks of the Fraser River. In addition to having a poop bag dispenser, there are about eight zillion signs asking you to leash your dog so I guess they're really serious about this here. Once you reach the Fraser River, however, the trail splits left and right. Follow the left split and you can walk up the Fraser, out of the park, until you reach Kanaka Landing Dock, where things get industrial.

If you take the right-hand split you stay in the park, cross a nice bridge at the mouth of Kanaka Creek, then on to a loop trail that brings you back to the bridge again.

How To Get There
Riverfront Park is accessed just east of where the Haney bypass meets up with the Lougheed Highway (#7), where the highway crosses Kanaka Creek. The parking lot is on the south side.

Hero's Rating: 🐾 🐾   **Human's Rating:** ★ ★ ★

Cliff Falls Park
Canyon Trail

Park Number	**154**
Trail Difficulty	2 - 3
Trail Condition	Excellent
Time	30 minutes

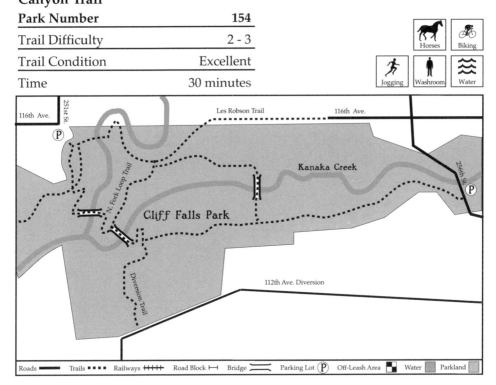

Cliff Falls Park is in a medium density forest. The Canyon Trail takes you from Cliff Falls Park to the Fish Hatchery. On the way you pass by parts of the canyon that are quite beautiful. A couple of times there is access to the creek. We didn't go to the hatchery, which I'm guessing is probably not a great place to take your dog.

How To Get There

From Dewdney Truck Road, turn south on 252nd. Follow this; it turns a couple times near the end, where there is a parking lot.

You can also approach this park from the south, taking 240th north from the Lougheed Highway (#7), right on 102nd Avenue, left on Industrial Avenue, another left on 248th Street, right on 108th Street, which jags to the right (110th Avenue) and left to become Lockwood, right on 112th Avenue, left on 252nd Street, right on 112th Avenue Diversion. Whew! You can see why the GVRD gives their directions to the other side of the park.

Hero's Rating: 🐾 🐾   **Human's Rating:** ★ ★ ★

North Fork Loop Trail

Park Number	154
Trail Difficulty	2 - 3
Trail Condition	Excellent
Time	20 minutes

Part of this trail is shared by horses. This trail takes you to the picnic area where you can see the falls that give the park its name. Wonderful. This is one of the only picnic areas I can think of that doesn't have "no dogs" signs plastered all over it. Not that this necessarily gives you access, however.

Hero's Rating: 🐾 🐾   **Human's Rating:** ★ ★ ★

Les Robson Trail

Park Number	154
Trail Difficulty	2 - 3
Trail Condition	Excellent
Time	30 minutes

You can access this very well groomed trail at the west end of 116th Avenue. Watch for horses on this trail.

Hero's Rating: 🐾   **Human's Rating:** ★ ★

Turkey Trot Trail

Park Number	154
Trail Difficulty	2 - 3
Trail Condition	Rustic
Time	15 minutes

A short jaunt down a path in a mainly deciduous forest. Unless you are willing to wade the creek, which is probably not advisable anyway, this is a very short but sweet little trail. Nice mossy trees.

How To Get There
Take 240th north from the Lougheed Highway, right on 102nd Avenue, left on Industrial Avenue, another left on 248th Street, another left on 110th Street. The trailhead is at the end of 110th.

Hero's Rating: 🐾   **Human's Rating:** ★

Lower Thorn Hill Trail

Park Number	154
Trail Difficulty	2 - 3
Trail Condition	Rustic
Time	15 - 30 minutes

Another short walk down a path in a mainly deciduous forest. Like Turkey Trot Trail, this trail has no bridge over the creek. Whichever side you come at it from will determine the length of your walk, the longer walks being on the north side of the creek.

How To Get There
Access off Fergusen Avenue by 112th Avenue on the south side, or off Trethewey Crescent, off 116th Avenue, on the north side.

Hero's Rating: 🐾   **Human's Rating:** ★

Matsqui Trail Regional Park (Matsqui)

Park Number	155
Trail Difficulty	1
Trail Condition	Excellent to fair
Time	up to 5 or 6 hours

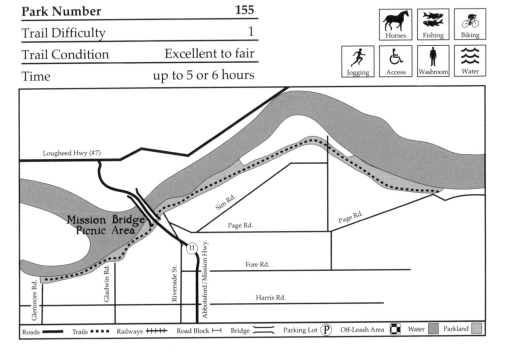

Matsqui Trail is a 10–km walk (one way) on a broad, flat well-groomed dyke with the Fraser River to the north and farmland to the south. For a good part of the walk, where the dyke is some distance from the river, there is also a lower trail nearer to the water. This trail is frequented by horses and can be very muddy.

The westernmost part of the park, Glenmore Road trailhead, is probably the least scenic, and the James Sewage Treatment Plant can augment the already odorous Fraser River mud to some effect.

The main development in the park is at the bridge where the #11 Highway goes over to Mission–the Mission Bridge Picnic Area, where there are campgrounds and fishing spots. A short way west of here there is a little pond and a grassy lawn.

Take care going over the train tracks just north of the park, or better yet, use the underpass.

The most scenic part of the park is the most easterly end. Here the development across the Fraser peters out and one can get a nice view up toward Harrison.

How To Get There

To get to the Mission Bridge Picnic Area: From the Trans-Canada Highway (#1) take exit #92 and go north on Highway #11 toward Mission. Turn left at Harris Road, then right on Riverside and look for the signs.

To get to the Glenmore Road trailhead: As above (Mission Bridge Picnic Area) to Harris, but go past Riverside and turn north on Glenmore

To get to the Page Road trailhead: As above (Mission Bridge Picnic Area) to Riverside, turn right on Page before the park entrance. Careful coming back. Some roads, like Fore, only enter the #11 going toward Mission.

Hero's Rating: 🐾 🐾 🐾   Human's Rating: ★ ★ ★ ★

Pitt-Addington Marsh Wildlife Management Area
(See **Addington Marsh** for Coquitlam side and **Grant Narrows Regional Park** for Pitt Meadows side)

Pitt Meadows Dykes (Pitt Meadows)

Park Number	156
Trail Difficulty	1
Trail Condition	Excellent to good
Time	Unlimited

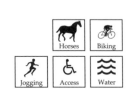

There are miles and miles of broad flat trails on the dykes along the Pitt and Fraser Rivers in Pitt Meadows. The dykes start on the Fraser River at Industrial at the south end of Harris, and run west from there. They travel right around the corner and head north up the Pitt River. I have been unable to travel the entire length of the dykes but they appear to go right up the Pitt to **Grant Narrows Regional Park** at Pitt Lake, with the interruption of **Alouette River**, also lined with dyke walks, but how far can you walk in one go?

Water quality in the Pitt River and the Fraser here is Good.

How To Get There

There are dykes all around Pitt Meadows, on the Pitt River, and on the Fraser. You can access the Fraser Dykes from the south end of Harris Road, or from the south end of Baynes by the airport. Harris crosses the Lougheed Highway just east of the Pitt River.

You can access the Pitt River Dykes at the north end of Harris, as well as a few other roads that reach the river, though parking can be a problem. A better idea is to park where Harris Road crosses the Alouette River. There are dykes here which you can walk to the Pitt, or drive up to **Grant Narrows Regional Park** .

Hero's Rating: 🐾 🐾 🐾   **Human's Rating:** ★ ★ ★

Widgeon Marsh Reserve Regional Park (Pitt Meadows)

Park Number	157
Trail Difficulty	2 - 4
Trail Condition	Rustic
Time	2 - 4 hours

Water

This park is mainly for canoeing, and it is actually in Coquitlam, but it is reached through Pitt Meadows, which is why it's in this section. You need a boat to get across the Pitt River to reach this park. You can rent a canoe in **Grant Narrows Regional Park**. If you canoe to the end of the slough, which is a body of water like a canal, there is a nice hike up a creek from where the camping site is.

Great park , but hard to get to for dog walking.

How To Get There

Follow Directions to **Grant Narrows Regional Park** .

Hero's Rating: 🐾 🐾 🐾   **Human's Rating:** ★ ★ ★

Park/Icon Cross-Reference Table

Park #	Off-Leash	Prohibited	Water	Phones	Washroom	Drinking	Access	Biking	Jogging	Swimming	Horses	Fishing
1		✓	✓		✓	✓	✓			✓		✓
2			✓				✓	✓				
3				✓			✓	✓	✓			
4		✓	✓	✓	✓	✓	✓	✓	✓			
5	✓	✓	✓	✓	✓	✓	✓	✓	✓	✓		✓
6		✓	✓	✓	✓	✓			✓		✓	
7		✓	✓	✓	✓	✓		✓	✓			
8		✓	✓	✓	✓	✓	✓	✓	✓			
9	✓	✓			✓	✓	✓					
10		✓	✓	✓	✓	✓	✓	✓				
11			✓									
12							✓					
13			✓									
14			✓					✓				
15		✓	✓	✓	✓	✓						
16			✓									
17			✓									
18		✓		✓	✓	✓	✓		✓			
19	✓		✓		✓				✓			
20							✓	✓	✓			
21		✓			✓	✓	✓					
22			✓					✓	✓		✓	
23			✓									
24			✓				✓	✓	✓			
25		✓	✓		✓		✓		✓			
26			✓						✓		✓	
27			✓									
28			✓									
29			✓									
30		✓	✓	✓	✓	✓						
31	✓	✓	✓				✓	✓	✓			
32			✓					✓				
33		✓	✓	✓	✓	✓	✓	✓	✓	✓	✓	✓
34						✓	✓					
35		✓	✓	✓	✓	✓	✓		✓			
36			✓	✓	✓	✓	✓					
37		✓	✓	✓	✓	✓	✓	✓	✓	✓		
38		✓	✓	✓	✓	✓	✓		✓		✓	✓
39			✓		✓	✓	✓	✓	✓		✓	
40			✓		✓							

Park/Icon Cross-Reference Table

Park #	Off-Leash	Prohibited	Water	Phones	Washroom	Drinking	Access	Biking	Jogging	Swimming	Horses	Fishing
41			●									
42		●	●									
43			●									
44			●					●	●		●	
45	●	●	●	●	●	●	●	●	●	●	●	
46	●	●	●	●	●	●					●	
47	●	●	●	●	●	●	●		●		●	●
48			●		●		●					●
49			●				●	●	●			●
50	●	●	●	●	●	●		●				●
51			●					●			●	
52		●	●	●	●	●	●	●	●			●
53		●	●		●		●	●	●	●		●
54		●										
55			●				●					
56	●		●									
57	●							●				
58	●							●			●	
59		●	●					●				
60	●	●	●	●	●	●	●	●	●		●	●
61			●	●	●	●	●		●			●
62	●	●	●		●	●						
63		●	●									
64		●	●									
65	●	●	●				●	●	●			
66		●	●	●	●	●		●				
67	●							●				
68	●		●					●				
69			●									
70	●			●	●	●		●				
71	●	●	●		●							
72	●		●									
73		●	●	●				●	●			●
74		●	●	●	●	●				●		●
75		●	●	●	●	●	●			●	●	●
76	●		●									
77		●										
78		●						●				
79	●		●									
80	●	●	●	●	●	●	●	●	●			●

Park/Icon Cross-Reference Table

Park #	Off-Leash	Prohibited	Water	Phones	Washroom	Drinking	Access	Biking	Jogging	Swimming	Horses	Fishing
81			✓				✓					
82	✓						✓	✓				
83			✓				✓					
84		✓	✓	✓	✓	✓	✓	✓				
85			✓	✓	✓	✓	✓	✓	✓	✓		
86		✓	✓	✓	✓	✓	✓					
87	✓		✓				✓	✓				
88	✓		✓									
89							✓	✓				
90	✓		✓				✓	✓				
91		✓	✓	✓	✓	✓	✓					
92			✓	✓	✓	✓	✓	✓	✓	✓		✓
93		✓	✓					✓				
94		✓	✓	✓	✓	✓	✓		✓			
95		✓	✓	✓	✓	✓	✓			✓		✓
96		✓	✓						✓			
97			✓		✓		✓		✓		✓	✓
98	✓		✓			✓	✓				✓	
99			✓		✓							
100		✓	✓		✓	✓	✓		✓			
101			✓				✓	✓				
102		✓			✓	✓	✓					
103			✓					✓				✓
104							✓					
105			✓					✓			✓	
106											✓	
107		✓			✓							
108		✓					✓		✓			
109			✓									
110			✓				✓					
111			✓									
112		✓	✓		✓		✓					
113			✓				✓	✓				
114	✓	✓	✓		✓		✓					
115	✓						✓					
116							✓					
117			✓				✓	✓	✓			
118			✓					✓	✓			
119	✓						✓					
120		✓	✓	✓	✓	✓	✓	✓	✓	✓		✓

Park/Icon Cross-Reference Table

Park #	Off-Leash	Prohibited	Water	Phones	Washroom	Drinking	Access	Biking	Jogging	Swimming	Horses	Fishing
121		✔	✔	✔	✔	✔	✔		✔	✔		
122	✔			✔	✔	✔	✔					
123		✔	✔	✔	✔	✔	✔	✔	✔	✔		
124			✔			✔	✔					✔
125			✔						✔			
126	✔						✔					
127			✔	✔	✔	✔	✔			✔		
128	✔	✔	✔	✔	✔			✔	✔	✔	✔	
129				✔	✔	✔	✔					
130		✔	✔	✔	✔	✔	✔	✔	✔	✔		✔
131			✔	✔			✔	✔	✔		✔	✔
132		✔	✔	✔	✔	✔	✔	✔	✔	✔	✔	✔
133		✔	✔	✔			✔	✔	✔			
134	✔	✔	✔	✔	✔	✔	✔	✔	✔	✔		✔
135	✔		✔	✔	✔	✔				✔		
136	✔		✔									
137	✔		✔									
138	✔	✔	✔	✔		✔	✔					
139		✔	✔	✔	✔		✔	✔	✔	✔	✔	
140	✔		✔									
141		✔	✔	✔	✔	✔		✔		✔		
142	✔		✔									
143	✔		✔		✔	✔				✔		✔
144	✔											
145	✔		✔									
146	✔											
147	✔		✔				✔	✔				
148	✔		✔									
149	✔	✔		✔	✔	✔				✔		
150	✔		✔		✔		✔	✔	✔		✔	
151			✔					✔				
152		✔	✔	✔	✔			✔		✔	✔	✔
153			✔	✔	✔		✔	✔	✔	✔		✔
154		✔	✔		✔		✔	✔	✔		✔	
155			✔		✔		✔	✔	✔		✔	✔
156			✔				✔	✔	✔		✔	
157			✔									

Appendix 2

Parks Boards

BC Provincial Parks	924-2200
Burnaby	294-7450
Coquitlam	933-6000
Delta	946-3293
Langley	532-7529
Langley City	530-3131
Maple Ridge	467-7346
New Westminster	526-4811
North Vancouver City	987-7529
North Vancouver District	990-3800
Pitt Meadows	465-2452
Port Coquitlam	927-7900
Port Moody	469-4555
Richmond	276-4107
Surrey	501-5050
Vancouver	257-8400
West Vancouver	925-7200
White Rock	541-2179

Other Groups

BC Hydro	528-2281
Burke Mountain Naturalists	942-7378
Burns Bog Conservation Society	572-0373
Canadian Wildlife Service	940-4700
Environment BC	582-5200
GVRD	432-6350
Inquiry BC	660-2421
Vancouver Airport Authority	276-1408

Dog Groups

Canine Good Citizen Program	939-0803
FIDO	538-8632
Vancouver Dog Owners Association	736-4640

Index

About the Authors

Ross W. Powell is a native of North Vancouver and has been hiking, camping, and canoeing around the Greater Vancouver area since he could balance on two feet. Recently acquiring a dog for the first time since childhood, he realized that a resource for dog-walkers was sadly lacking and so set out to produce one.

Ross has worked in Television as a Researcher, as a Production Manager in Special Events production, and as a Stage Manager, including a four-year period with the Vancouver Symphony.

Hero is a three-year-old purebred Golden Retriever. He loves splashing in water and going for walks more than anything else in the world and hates retrieving. When at home Hero enjoys playing with his cats, Monet and Chagall.

Notes

Notes

Notes

Notes

Notes

Notes

Notes

Notes

Notes